to Linda & Mike —
with gratitude for
all the memories &
blessings —
with love

Rabbi Karen Fox
October 2014

Broken Tablets

Although Moses shattered the first set of tablets containing the Ten Words when he saw the Israelites worshipping the golden calf, even the broken pieces were deposited in the ark. Once a vessel for God's teaching, they remain forever sacred, forever whole.

הלוחות ושברי לוחות מונחין בארון

(*Menachot* 99a)

Broken Tablets

Restoring the Ten Commandments and Ourselves

EDITED BY RACHEL S. MIKVA

Jewish Lights Publishing
Woodstock, Vermont

Broken Tablets: Restoring the Ten Commandments and Ourselves

© 1999 by Rachel S. Mikva

Permission to reprint material from the following sources is gratefully acknowledged:

Translations from *The Tanakh: The New JPS Translation According to the Traditional Hebrew Text,* copyright © 1985 by the Jewish Publication Society. Used by permission. Page 5, quote from *Seek My Face, Speak My Name* by Arthur Green. Reprinted by permission of the publisher, Jason Aronson, Inc., Northvale, NJ © 1994. Page 19, parable paraphrased from "The Condition of Jewish Belief" by Arnold Jacob Wolf, *Commentary* 1966 (August) 2:42. Reprinted by permission of the publisher. Chapter 3, quotations from the Book of Job from *The Book of Job* copyright © 1979 and 1987 by Stephen Mitchell. HarperCollins Publishers, Inc. Reprinted by permission. Page 46, quote from *Likrat Shabbat* by Sidney Greenberg, published by Hartman House (1985). Page 64, quote from *The Measure of Our Success* by Marian Wright Edelman, published by Beacon Press (1993). Page 82, quote from "And My Brother Said Nothing" by Amir Gilboa from *The Penguin Book of Hebrew Verse.*

Library of Congress Cataloging-in-Publication Data

Broken tablets: restoring the Ten Commandments and ourselves
/ edited by Rachel Mikva.
p.   cm.
Includes bibliographical references.
ISBN 1-58023-066-0 (hc)
1. Ten commandments. I. Mikva, Rachel, 1960–
BM520.75B75   1999
296.3'6—dc21   99–40417
                                            CIP

First Edition

10 9 8 7 6 5 4 3 2

Manufactured in the United States of America

Jacket design: Bridgett Taylor
Text design: Josh Silverman : schwadesign
Typesetting: Reuben Kantor, QEP Design

Published by Jewish Lights Publishing
A Division of LongHill Partners, Inc.
Sunset Farm Offices, Route 4, P.O. Box 237
Woodstock, Vermont 05091
Tel: (802)457-4000 Fax: (802)457-4004
www.jewishlights.com

For Rabbi Arnold Jacob Wolf,
Our teacher, colleague, and friend.
Your questions leave us breathless, and you
know better than to give the answers.

לבך יהגה תבונה, פיך ידבר חכמות

... עיניך יאירו במאור תורה

May your heart always be so wise,
your mouth speak wisdom,
and your eyes ever shine with the light of Torah.

(Berachot 17a)

Contents

Acknowledgments   ix

Introduction   xi
BY RABBI LAWRENCE KUSHNER

Perspectives on the Ten Words   xvii
BY RABBI RACHEL S. MIKVA

1. The First Commandment   1
I, *Adonai* your God, [am the one] who brought you out
of the land of Egypt, from a slavehouse.
FIRST WORDS   3
I [Am the One]
BY RABBI EUGENE B. BOROWITZ

2. The Second Commandment   15
Have no other god before Me....
FIRST WORDS   17
No Other
BY RABBI ZALMAN M. SCHACHTER-SHALOMI

3. The Third Commandment   25
You shall not lift up the name of *Adonai* your God for
vain purpose, for *Adonai* will not clear one who uses
the Name in vain.
FIRST WORDS   27
Thou Shalt Not Take the Name
BY RABBI NANCY FUCHS-KREIMER

4. The Fourth Commandment   41
Remember the Sabbath day and keep it holy....
FIRST WORDS   43
The Meaning of Shabbat: A Virtual Domain in Time
BY RABBI LAWRENCE A. HOFFMAN

5. The Fifth Commandment   **59**
Honor your father and mother that your days may be prolonged on the soil that *Adonai* your God is giving you.

FIRST WORDS   61
I Was Young, and I Have Also Grown Older
BY LEONARD FEIN

6. The Sixth Commandment   **73**
You shall not murder.

FIRST WORDS   75
Undoing Creation
BY RABBI LEVI WEIMAN-KELMAN

7. The Seventh Commandment   **85**
You shall not commit adultery.

FIRST WORDS   87
Sacred Boundaries
BY RABBI PETER S. KNOBEL

8. The Eighth Commandment   **97**
You shall not steal.

FIRST WORDS   99
A Bit of a Thief
BY RABBI RICHARD N. LEVY

9. The Ninth Commandment   **109**
You shall not answer against your neighbor as
a false witness.

FIRST WORDS   111
Competing Values
BY RABBI LAURA GELLER

10. The Tenth Commandment   **123**
You shall not covet your neighbor's house. You shall not
covet your neighbor's wife, or his male or female slave,
or his ox or his ass, or anything that is your neighbor's.

FIRST WORDS   125
Desire
BY DR. MENACHEM KELLNER

Ten More Words   **133**
BY RABBI ARNOLD JACOB WOLF
Sources and Notes   **137**
About the Contributors   **145**

Acknowledgments

I had the privilege of working with Rabbi Arnold Jacob Wolf in Chicago, just after I was ordained. For four years (and beyond), he challenged me and supported me, helping me to grow not only as a rabbi, but also as a Jew.

While my thanks go above all to him for all that he has taught me, thus making this book possible, I am deeply grateful to many others as well for their guidance and help. Rabbi Larry Kushner undertook to shepherd this project, generously sharing his wisdom, humor, and experience. My friend Rabbi Betsy Torop read the manuscript with eyes just different enough than my own, and her suggestions were of great value. Stuart Matlins, Arthur Magida, Jennifer Goneau, Sandra Korinchak, and Martha McKinney at Jewish Lights invested their time, talent, and enthusiasm to bring the project to completion. Leila Linares patiently typed and retyped, phoned, faxed, mailed and e-mailed to get all the pieces to come together.

To all of the authors, who graced us with their profound learning and creative minds, and then waited with messianic patience for the volume to come to fruition — thank you.

To Mark, Jacob, and Keren, who grace my life with love and joy, and teach me the meaning of faithfulness — I love you always and forever.

Introduction

LAWRENCE KUSHNER

Rolled into one almost, but not entirely, soundless seed, like a coil of deoxyribonucleic acid containing some kind of secret genotype for all creation, or maybe an Einsteinian singularity into which is stuffed all matter, energy, space, and time, or like just an ordinary jack-in-the-box, ready at the touch of a child's finger to explode, surprise, delight, and terrify — the divine voice is condensed into the Hebrew letter *alef*.

Creation begins with the Hebrew letter *bet* of "*bereshit* (בראשית), In the beginning," but what God says at Sinai begins with the letter *alef* of "*anochi* (אנכי), I am." *Bet* is the second letter of the alphabet and also stands for the number two. *Alef* is the first letter and represents the number one. Creation — it is obvious to anyone with eyes and ears — is more than one. It is a teeming multiplicity of apparent contradictions. But God's utterance at Sinai, though riddled with infinite meaning, is somehow one. That's what we're talking about here in this book: the content and the experience and the unity of what happened at Sinai.

Soundless Alef

> Rabbi Eleazar taught: In these ten statements are embodied all the commandments in the Torah, decrees and punishments, cleanness and uncleanness, branches and roots, trees and plants, heaven and earth, sea and the deeps. For the Torah is the Name of the Holy One. Just as the Name of the Holy One is embodied in the ten utterances, so the Torah also is embodied in the ten utterances. *(Zohar II 90a-b)*

What *really* happened at that mountain in the wilderness? Did God actually speak in real words? Did God write something in black fire on white fire? Did Moses really see it? Did the Jews really hear it? Such questions jiggle the core of Western religion. Consider the implications, for instance, if Moses simply concocted the whole thing or if those words on the tablets are literally God's words. Are these two options mutually exclusive?

According to the most popularly rehearsed tradition, God gave Moses the entire Torah at Mount Sinai. Others, unwilling or unable to reconcile some of the obvious inconsistencies with such an assertion, claim that God gave Moses only the Ten Commandments themselves. The Ten thus become a metaphor for the Torah and thereby for *all* divine revelation.

These ten get further distilled into five. As our commentators noted long ago, the second five (not to commit murder, adultery, theft, and perjury, or to covet) describe and regulate the sphere of the inter-human, what happens between one person and another. The first five (I'm God, not to commit idolatry or to trash God's Name, to revere the Sabbath and parents) speak instead of our relationship with God. (Parents, being our link with life and God, are number five and could properly go at the bottom of the first table or at the top of the second.) As we read in the *midrash,* "The second Five Commandments were intended to be paired off with the first Five Commandments." The *Zohar* is even more explicit. "In these five utterances everything is contained. In the [first] five utterances are embodied [the latter] five others. Indeed, there are five within five..."

Dividing the ten into two sets of five like this has some fascinating implications. Surely one of the most insignificant miracles in all of Jewish tradition originates in how the letters were physically hewn onto the tablets. Each letter, we are told, was carved *all the way through* the stone so that someone could actually see through to the other side. But there are two letters, *samech* (ס) and final *mem* (ם), both of which completely enclose a space (like the letters "d" or "o" in English). If they were carved all the way through, there would be no way to support their inner stone. This was accomplished by a minor miracle. The stone just hung there, miraculously suspended in space!

Less whimsically, what could it mean that the words were carved clear through to the other side? Perhaps there was only one tablet. Read from one side, the words describe what we owe God. From the other side they describe what we must do for one another. And it's the same thing! By the time the letters are carved through to the other side, the meaning of the words is transformed. The miracle may be that it is a kind of lapidary palindrome: Viewed from either side, the readings are coherent, compelling, even infinite.

The first five can be further condensed into the first two. Along comes the Talmud and, using gematria (the ancient system of assigning each Hebrew letter a numerical equivalent), asks a question: Why do the Hebrew letters for the word "Torah" (*tav* ת, 400 + *vav* ו, 6 + *resh* ר, 200 + *hey* ה, 5) total only 611 — just 2 short of 613, the magic number of all the commandments in the Torah? The answer given there is that "*Torah tsivah lanu Moshe,* Moses gave us a Torah" (611 commandments), but two we heard directly from God, "*mipi haGevurah,* from the mighty mouth itself." And those two are the first two: *I am God* and *You shall have no idols.*

In other words, what we learned at Sinai was about Self and other, surely the touchstone for any religion. Without you, I cannot be. Only through your *otherness* and individuality can I come into being. But I cannot voluntarily bring myself into being. I can, however, bring you into being by acknowledging your individuality and, in so doing, I effectively participate in my own creation. But only as long as I *only* think about cherishing your otherness and never about my self!

These first two can be fused into the first one: I am God. But this one is not even a commandment; it is literally only an utterance, a declaration, "I am the One who brought you out of slavery in Egypt." "I am the One of freedom." "I am the One who frees people from what enslaves them." God effectively gets us all together at Sinai and says: This is who I am. And we say: That's all we need to know. Surely this realization contains the germ of all Torah that is to follow. As the philosopher Alexander Altmann once observed, "God and man's self are essentially one — this recognition forms the perennial theme of all mysticism... [and]

finding God and worshipping Him is but another way of saying that we have found our Self.... God is in the Self but the Self is not god...."

The content of this first utterance is, in turn, distilled into its first word, "*anochi*, I." God spoke all right, but all God said was the first person pronoun singular: I. And this means that if the universe can utter the first person pronoun singular, it must have a self. After all, what is a self if not the name we give to that capacity of our psyches that somehow persuades everyone that all our otherwise discordant, mutually exclusive, contradictory thoughts, feelings, and actions are part of a unified personality? Indeed we can also reasonably read the Hebrew — in which the verb "to be" is only inferred in the present tense — not as "I am the Lord, your God" but as, "I *is* the Lord, your God."

There is still more. According to a teaching of Rabbi Mendl Torum of Rymanov (d. 1814) and recounted by Gershom Scholem, the first word, *anochi,* is itself contained within its first letter, the letter *alef.* And this letter is the first letter of the Hebrew alphabet, a letter, which as we have already noted according to gematria, means the number one. For this reason the *Zohar* says that this *alef* also plays a role in God's unification. Here is a letter whose only sound is the noise of the larynx clicking into gear and that, as Scholem suggests, must be the mother of all articulate speech. It represents the softest yet still audible sound in the universe — so soft that any other sound will drown it out.

So, in one sense, the pages that follow are an attempt to elucidate the meaning of and amplify the sound of that first letter, *alef.*

My Teacher

The following essays were written by people whose lives and teaching have been influenced by Arnold Jacob Wolf. They are all expressions of respect and reverence for one of the great lights of our generation. It was my privilege to learn as his apprentice at Congregation Solel in Highland Park, Illinois from 1969 to 1971. I remember the first time I ever watched him teach the Ten Commandments. It was nothing short of thrilling to observe a great rabbi teach something everyone was expected to know but no one had ever been taught. He had the chutzpah to say that there really was a God and that God really commanded us to follow the Ten Commandments. Highly educated, religious liberals sat on the edge of their seats. Wolf said, glowering over the class, "That's right. All the old lies are true. Go home and read the Bible!" His teaching was and always will be for me a revelation, a challenge, a hope.

May God hold him so that his eyes be undimmed and his vigor unabated (Deuteronomy 34:7).

Perspectives on the Ten Words

RACHEL S. MIKVA

"Broken, are they? And *we* are going to fix them?" It was Gene Borowitz on the telephone, and he didn't like the title of the book.

Well, yes, the Ten Commandments frequently do seem broken. We steal. We covet. We fail to honor our parents in ways large and small. Most of us don't bow down to small clay statues anymore, but certainly we make many things in our lives more important than God. The Sabbath, it seems, has never been kept as it was intended. Our sages believed that if we could observe it properly for just one or two weeks in a row, the messiah would come. We are still waiting...

Besides, doesn't the Torah itself say that Moses, furious at the shameful and shameless worship of the golden calf, smashes the tablets that were inscribed by the finger of God? At the foot of the same mountain where the people experience God's revelation, where they promise to obey — they break the commandments, and Moses breaks the tablets.

Of course, the Rabbis pick up the pieces, as they always do. With the power of their interpretive imagination, they rescue the fragments from the dust bin of religious history and deposit them in the ark with the whole tablets written later. That's what the sages hear in God's instruction to Moses in Deuteronomy (10:2) to place *them* in the ark: both the intact tablets of stone and the seemingly useless pieces. The Rabbis have a point to make, as they usually do. The shattered tablets are like a scholar who has forgotten his learning, they say, who must still be treated with reverence for all that he once contained and transmitted. I wonder who they're thinking of...

In the process of protecting the senior citizens of the scholar class, they open for us a more significant possibility. The words of God are never broken. Even if we violate their integrity, we cannot vitiate their power. As evidence, we can cite the vast percentage of

XVII

Christians and Jews who affirm the importance of the Ten Commandments (even if they can only name six or seven of them).

However, as Martin Buber teaches, the word of God comes not to be believed in, but to be done. The Ten Words count in the ways they shape our lives and here, the Jewish tradition again opens a path before us. In turning Torah over and over again, the Ten Words teach a multitude of things, some of which we have not even yet imagined, few of which we have mastered. Along with the new voices of the authors of these essays, I have added the voice of traditional and other modern commentary in the "First Words" preceding each chapter. Together, they challenge us to restore the words to wholeness by our actions — deeds of heart and mind and body.

It has been taught: All the interpretations ever uttered or ever to be spoken were disclosed by God to Moses on Mt. Sinai. This is the oral Torah. It may mean that they were talking about you, about what you will discover and teach in your lifetime. Attach yourself to the story. Listen to the word. Accept the command. In so doing, you will restore to fullness what God knew about you long ago.

How Were the Ten Commandments Arranged?

Five on one tablet and five on the other.

On one tablet it is written: *I am the Lord your God.* And opposite it on the other tablet is written: *You must not murder.* Whoever sheds blood has destroyed a reflection of God, for we are created in the Divine image. Imagine a king of flesh and blood, who erects statues of his likeness and stamps his image on coins to remind people of his role. If the people begin to rebel against the king, they cannot strike at his person, but they may tear down the statues and deface the coins. When we murder, we destroy the image of God.

On one tablet it is written: *Have no other god before Me.* And opposite it on the other tablet is written: *You must not commit adultery.* Our religion and our marriage both require fidelity. If we worship idols, it is as if we commit adultery, because we break our covenant with God.

On one tablet it is written: *You must not lift up the name of Adonai, your God, for vain purpose.* And opposite it on the other tablet is written: *You must not steal.* This suggests that one who steals will in the end also swear falsely in God's name to deny it.

On one tablet it is written: *Remember the Sabbath day and keep it holy.* And opposite it on the other tablet is written: *You must not bear false witness.* If we profane the Sabbath, it is as though we testify: God did not create the world! Nor did God ordain a day of rest and sanctification.

On one tablet it is written: *Honor your father and mother.* And opposite it on the other tablet is written: *You must not covet your neighbor's wife.* Our coveting can lead to illicit affairs and complex relationships or families, in which the children end up unable to give both of their parents proper respect, or may be unsure to whom that honor is due.

Some rabbis, however, insist that all ten pronouncements are written on both tablets. Since there are at least two slightly different versions of these commandments — the encounter on Mount Sinai in Exodus Chapter 20, and Deuteronomy Chapter 5 when Moses repeats the essential teachings for the people — some commentators suggest that one version was written on each tablet, and both were given together.

Utterances or Commandments

In Hebrew, they are called *aseret hadibrot,* the ten utterances — not the Ten Commandments. The term "decalogue," borrowed from Greek (*deka logoi,* or ten words), is the most accurate English translation, even if it does sound similar to the tongue-in-cheek translation, "the ten suggestions." Whether they are commandments, words, or suggestions, if they manage to speak in God's voice, that which is spoken is that which must be.

Were the Israelites Coerced?

And they stood under the mountain (Exodus 19:17). Rabbi Abdimi bar Hama bar Hasa said: This teaches that the Holy One of Blessing held the mountain over their heads like an inverted cask, and said to them, "If you accept the Torah, all will be well; if not, this is where you will be buried." Rabbi Aha bar Ya'akov objected to this interpretation: This furnishes a strong protest against the Torah. We cannot be coerced into accepting our covenantal obligations!

Divine blackmail is a fanciful image, but it reflects the stakes the Rabbis felt were involved: All of creation depended upon the people's willingness to take on the *mitzvot.* When Jeremiah spoke in our name: "Were it not for My covenant by day and night, I would not have created heaven and earth" (a dramatic translation of Jeremiah 33:25), the Rabbis took him seriously.

Standing at Sinai

When the Holy One gave the Torah, no bird chirped, no fowl flew, no ox lowed, not one angel stirred its wing or sang its song. The sea did not roar. Creatures did not speak. The whole world was hushed into breathless silence. It was then that the voice went forth: "I am the Lord your God…"

With each and every word of the Holy One, the entire world was filled with a unique fragrance of spice. Each and every word broke into seventy languages as it spread, filling the earth with the teaching of God.

Torah was given in the wilderness so all could receive it, and any one who ever did or ever will embrace the covenant, stood at Sinai, saw the thunder and the lightning, smelled the fragrance, and heard the word in a way that he or she could understand.

Is There a Logic to Their Structure?

Jewish tradition notes that on the first tablet, the pronouncements are concerned primarily with obligations to God *(bein adam leMakom)*. On the second tablet, they focus on our obligations to each other *(bein adam lechavero)*. The bridge between these two realms is honoring our parents. Like God, they are our creators. They also nurture and sustain us, instruct us, command us, chasten us, and ultimately let us grow into our own lives. These experiences shape both our image of God and our understanding of societal obligations.

The Roman emperor Hadrian asked Rabbi Joshua ben Chananyah why God's name is not even mentioned in any of the commandments on the second tablet. The sage answered: It is just as you place your statue or insignia on almost every building in the empire, but not on outhouses and such places. God associates the Divine name with the commandments on the first tablet, speaking of faith, honor and the Sabbath. We cannot associate God's name, however, with heinous sins such as murder, adultery, theft, false testimony, and covetous desire.

More important than the structure of the commandments, however, is their radical objective: trying to unite a community around common obligations rather than common interests.

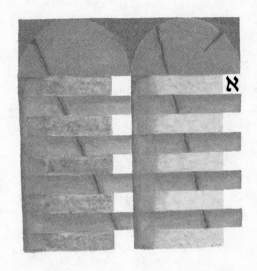

one

אָנֹכִי יי אֱלֹהֶיךָ

אֲשֶׁר הוֹצֵאתִיךָ מֵאֶרֶץ מִצְרַיִם

מִבֵּית עֲבָדִים.

I, *Adonai* your God,
[am the one]
who brought you out of the land of Egypt,
from a slavehouse.

translation, Eugene Borowitz

The First Commandment

How can God command belief?

It is not clear whether "I, *Adonai* your God" is a commandment at all. A *mitzvah* (commandment) must be governed by free will and choice; faith is not. How can God insist that we accept the Divine reality and rule? What if we cannot believe? Some commentators suggest that it could simply be a preface (albeit an essential one) to the actual commands. Their authority depends on our faith in a Commander.

A parable: A new king came to rule, but refused to pass any laws. His advisors urged him to assert his rule more visibly. But he insisted, "They must first come to accept me as their king. Then they will know that the laws I give them are for blessing."

Yet Moses Maimonides calls it the first among *mitzvot*, the pillar upon which all religion and science rest. We are called upon to believe in God and to know that there is a first (Divine) cause. Perhaps it is commanded the way any necessary thing is commanded.

Ma'aseh shehayah... It once happened

that a young man went to study with the Maggid of Mezritch. He stayed away a long time, until he found what he was looking for. Returning home, his angry father-in-law demanded to know what he could possibly have learned that would justify neglecting his family.

"I learned that there is a God."

His father-in-law was not sure whether to laugh or yell at this foolish man. He summoned the maid and asked, "Is there a God?"

"Of course, sir," she laughed nervously. "Everyone believes in God."

"You see!" he bellowed at his son-in-law. "You deserted your family for Mezritch to learn something that even an illiterate maid could have told you!"

The young man remained calm. "She *says* there is a God, but in Mezritch I learned to *know* there is a God."

What did the people hear at Sinai?

Most commentators conclude that the people heard only the first two utterances.

Nachmanides points out that the first two are phrased in the first person, with God speaking directly. The others speak about God, as if Moses is reporting what God said. In the Talmud, the Rabbis play with gematria, a system of interpretation in which each Hebrew letter also stands for a number. Jewish tradition enumerates 613 commandments in the Torah; the word *Torah* (תורה) itself has the numerical value of 611. Moses taught 611 *mitzvot;* the other two the people heard for themselves.

Still, there is not complete agreement. Rashi insists that the people heard the first two of these utterances word for word. Maimonides argues that they heard only the sound, unintelligible without Moses' help.

Franz Rosenzweig, a modern philosopher, suggests that what the people received at Sinai was a revelation of God's overwhelming presence and love. From that experience, they translated what they understood of God's will into commandments, teachings to guide their lives. Perhaps this idea is not so different than a much older interpretation:

> All they heard was the first letter, the א of אנכי (*Anochi*, I). But it is a silent letter! Yes, what the people heard at Sinai was the sound of the Holy One of Blessing opening a gateway, as if opening a mouth to begin to speak. The beginning of a conversation — and it was enough.

Wouldn't we know that it is God who speaks?

It is necessary to identify God as the One who appeared in various guises — a man of war at the Sea, an elderly scholar full of mercy at Sinai: "I alone was in Egypt, I alone was at the Sea, I alone was at Sinai. It was I in the past and it will be I in the future." It is assumed from the very beginning that our experience of God is fragmented, incomplete, even contradictory. We experience God in different ways at different times in our lives. Each person apprehends God according to his or her own capacity and experience.

The very first teaching then must be: It is I. I am the One God of your life. When we can see our experiences as parts of the Whole, and share with each other what we have learned of the Divine, we begin to understand the unity of God.

Why mention Egypt?

Ibn Ezra wonders why God chooses to be revealed as redeemer from Egyptian slavery, rather than creator of the entire universe. He reasons that only philosophers will understand God within creation or the science of thought. For them, "I am the Lord" would be sufficient. Most of us, however, need compelling first-hand experience in order to believe, which for the Israelites was their rescue from Egypt.

Benno Jacob asks why the text bothers to say "from the house of bondage," when Egypt is already mentioned and the nature of that experience is all too well ingrained on the minds and hearts of the people. Perhaps, he notes, it comes to remind us how important one's perspective can be. Egypt was the center of ancient culture, famed for its pyramids and art. For Israel, however, it was nothing more than a house of serfs. The insight of this nineteenth to twentieth century German scholar speaks to every time and place. While the United States is known for many great things, for instance, it was a house of bondage for Africans and a house of conquerors for Native Americans. Even today, its status as a great nation depends on your point of view.

Seeking God

> I was ready to be sought by those who did not
> ask for Me; I was ready to be found by those
> who did not seek Me; I said "Here I am, here I
> am" to a nation that did not call My name.
> (Isaiah 65:1)

God is both immanent and transcendent — high and exalted beyond this world, yet present within history. How could God

5

take us out of Egypt? As Arthur Green wrote in *Seek My Face,*
Speak My Name:

> The divine presence is incarnate in all the world.
> God is *ruach kol basar,* the spirit that resides in
> all flesh. That presence may be brought to con-
> sciousness in the mind of every human who is
> open to it, as it may be blocked out and negated
> entirely by the closing of the human heart, by
> cruelty, or by the denial of God's image. The
> *Shechinah,* the divine presence in our world,
> does not dwell where she is not wanted.

— *Rachel S. Mikva*

I [Am the One]

EUGENE B. BOROWITZ

"I"

Someone is talking to me. I am not standing at Sinai and I hear no voice. All I have is a text, but that turns out to be not as inert as we might think letters on a page or screen are. As long as I can remember, the text has been read, chanted, for my (and others') benefit. Even when I am alone with the text, the voice of the reader/chanter dimly sounds in me, bringing the words to me as a living address. Mostly, I see/hear it in context, embraced in the story of the Jewish people's memory of what happened — and understood by them and me to be most sacred. Even read in utter silence, as happened just a moment ago when I prepared to begin writing these words, it came to me as address. (And were Jewishness not central to my being and were I only another reasonably sensitive participant in western civilization, the words would still come to me as someone speaking to me.)

Who is talking? As yet, I don't know. Normally I would look to see where the sound is coming from or concentrate on its timber so that the first few syllables of this Hebrew "I" might identify the speaker. But while the very word "I" makes the act of address plain, there is no one to look at and no sound pattern to identify. And in all the times that I have read/heard this text, there has been no vision or sound connected with this "I" that I might now bring to this hearing.

Yet the word, which in its unadorned articulation seems so devoid of content, is, after all, the mysterious distance/nearness I/we share with You.

You — not Moses, not one of the other prophets — You Yourself speak. You present Yourself to me and to us, momentarily making the Far-Off-One the Here-Near-One, approaching as close as our retinas or eardrums. To have been so visited, even if only in paltry recapitulation, dignifies us unalienably.

You tell us Your name, and by it we come close enough to glimpse who You are and are thereby debarred from ever presuming to call you by it. We mean to cherish Your name by avoiding it, by calling You other things instead, none of them unproblematic. Our oldest euphemism, "Lord," now distorts our sense of nearness to You and is too gender-heavy to reflect the breadth of experience with You. Those today whose self-confidence disdains these old bounds and who assert their intimacy with ultimacy by readily calling You by name are nonetheless guessing how to pronounce it as, tradition says, the High Priest did each year in ancient Jerusalem. Yet just when the climactic moment of utterance came on Yom Kippur day, the Levite choirs increased their volume so no distinct sound could be heard. Nonetheless, the very notion that the High Priest was calling You by name shook us enough that everyone in the Temple threw themselves to the ground before You.

Though we are confined to English, Your name still puzzles and dazzles us. No hint of the sacred four Hebrew consonants is found in the Indo-European root *gheu* (to call, invoke) from which our Germanic-English "God" derives and it surely is more an abstraction than a proper name. Nonetheless, some today reflect their Hebraic awe in their English usage. Reverence for God suggests not fully spelling out the word, so "G-d" or "Gd" become distinctive signs of North American Jewish piety. With disrespect for God rife, believers can well cherish these signs of honest concern. Yet as with so many symbols, a shadow cannot be avoided. Deforming Your title/name seems a curious act of demonstrating regard for You. Does the *yetser hara* (the evil inclination, which is always in tension with our inclination for good) of otherwise inadmissible doubt here subtly infiltrate piety and, in every repetition do to "God" what the Rabbis said to do to idols so that, once they are defaced, statues might no longer be offensive to the Jewish soul?

• • •

"I, *Adonai* your God…"

"My" God? Surely *Adonai* is God of everyone and everything. Why then this surprising singular: "thy God?" Why this personal address to me — or not to me or any other individual, but to the people? Your reach here is clearly corporate, communal, national, but in all these Words, You address me/us individually. In pre-enlightenment days and certainly back in Bible times, people did not suffer from today's fearsome gap between the self-legislating I and its society. Rather the self and its group so imperceptibly merged into one another that modern scholars must speculate whether the biblical poet's "I" refers to a person, the nation, or, more likely, both at once in shifting emphasis. So by meaning me, you mean all the children of the covenant, each one preciously an individual to You.

Nonetheless, the singular "thy" comes as a two-fold imperative. The nation, in responding to *Adonai,* must not forget the supreme value of the single self. Only as individuals one by one, doing what *Adonai* requires of Israel, can the nation fulfill its covenantal responsibility. I must not forget that though the Jewish people has an existence independent of me, until I (and other individual Jews) carry out the commandments incumbent upon me (us) as one of all-Israel, it cannot be the Jewish people God is calling it to be. And that begins with knowing that *Adonai* is "my" God in a most personal and intimate way. Temperament, training, soul, experience, endowment — all mix to make me just who I am and the way I go about being/becoming me. You ask me, *Adonai,* by addressing me personally, to fulfill the common duty of all-Israel as just the me I am — that is, in terms of my unique self. To be sure, I speak here with some hesitation, knowing how much I have been affected by the special prominence modernity has given to the self. Yet our people has long cherished the many individualists and idiosyncratics who served You over its centuries, and it has lovingly transmitted their stories to us. I/we respond to Your evocative address to the nation as a collection of single selves by carrying on our uncommon Jewish blend of individualism and corporate concern.

"I, *Adonai* your God, [am the one] who…"

The English translation has now betrayed me badly enough that I must intrude upon its flow with bracketed words. Already in my

9

problems rendering the sense of the previous Hebrew word, *Elohecha* (your God), the non-Hebraic soul of the English language made itself felt. Its "your" might well suggest a Hebraic ambiguity of singular or plural address. So I had recourse to the archaic "thy" to make the singularity of the Hebrew fully evident. Were it not for the Hebrew *asher,* which here means "who," the translation might have proceeded as the Hebrew does, without introducing a verb speaking of existence, "am."

What shall we make of the fact that, compared to western languages, Hebrew seems to take existence for granted — or at least does not often see the need to introduce words to refer to being?

Shall we say that existence does not seem so remarkable to the Hebrews that they find it worth mentioning? Or is it the opposite: Non-being is so contrary to their way of facing reality that the wonder of existence becomes almost as ineffable as God? Whatever the case, without *asher* I could have rendered the text without an interpolation this way: I, *Adonai* your God, brought you out of the land of Egypt, from a slavehouse. But by saying *asher,* the text stresses the connection between "I, *Adonai* your God" and "brought you out..." requiring something like my "[am the one]" to render its sense in English.

Shall I now simply pass over the fact that I have added some words to the Ten that the Torah declares God said directly to the people of Israel at Sinai? At least I have called my act to your attention, inviting you to join me in wondering about how much else I, in my English-shaped thinking about Judaism, have reconfigured its message while transmitting it. Or should we be consoled that there has never been a moment when the Hebrew language stood still long enough to equip its words with some kind of prime, pure, essential meaning? Does not the biblical record show and our linguistic experience affirm that words and their combinations never fix into one perfect meaning that all else adulterates? Meaning abides in these shifting connotations in as obvious and mysterious a way as I remain me while going through the passages of my life. In translation as in life, we can only strive for ever greater integrity.

"I, *Adonai* your God, [am the one] who brought you out..."

Of course You did. But I mean no disrespect by quietly remembering that if I hadn't walked on my own two feet I might still be in the land of Goshen. And, while the text doesn't make much of the minutiae of the journeying — relying, I assume, on our great Jewish talent for complaining — it isn't difficult to imagine what daily activity was like when Your cloud lifted, signaling that we were to fold up our tents, repack the goods, get the family together, find our place in the march, and start another trudge. The daily mood, I would guess, was less the high that accompanied Your constant presence than the tedium of one foot after another and the hope against hope that today the ever-lurking problems wouldn't surface and further complicate our lives.

That recital in no way mitigates the wonder You did. Whenever we could lift our spirits so weighed down by each day's demands, we knew we could never have gotten out of Egypt solely on our own. It was as mighty an empire as the world had ever known. Why should they lose all our slave power so necessary for their awe-inspiring, slave-killing projects? Moses' charisma and group cohesion wouldn't have kept us going for very long. No wonder historians, pointing to the absence of confirming external evidence, have argued that although the exodus story is a marvelous national saga, it never happened: "History" doesn't work that way, at least not if you abide by the secular conventions of the academy that rule God out of their kind of "history." Our people, impressed by the continual improbabilities of what has happened to us over the centuries — not the least being that, against all odds, we are still around — knows that again and again God has showed up and, one way or another, brought us out. Not without our putting one foot in front of another, to be sure. Partnership, not unilateral action, has been our sense of God as taker-out but with no confusion over who was the Senior Partner in the process.

Not all the great faiths that call You "one" proclaim You, as do we, Bringer-out. They apparently believe that to involve You in history this way is to compromise Your purity or the fullness of Your being. We, who identify You not only as creator but as the one who called creation "good" — though flawed since the primal parents were chased out of Eden — know You only as the participating One. To us, one sign of Your greatness is that You are involved with us (and others) and by such interaction do not compromise Your superlative status. As the daily prayer epitomizes You: *Melech-ozer-umoshia-umagen* (King-helper-and saver-and shielder).

The very one who is Most High is also the one who bends down low, not one without the other. And because You continue to be Bringer-out, we are a hoping people.

Not unproblematically so. If Your greatness rendered You neutral toward us, we would not have the problem of evil. Why should a universe indifferent to us not occasionally (or more often) erupt into evil? Why expect anything else? Our spirituality begins with wonder at how beneficent we find creation — that is, when we stop taking it for granted (as if there were no Grantor). That is particularly true when, after some depressing personal situation or historical calamity, Your help has brought us out once again. More than a hundred Jewish generations have wondered why You do not intervene more often or more quickly, how You can let the people of Israel suffer long years of Egyptian slavery before bringing them out. And the last couple of generations have brought us a new level of anguish over Your inscrutable time schedule. Yet we have also seen incomparable evidences of Your saving hand, though they cannot be said — vile thought — to compensate for the suffering that preceded them. A generation back some said You were dead, a curiously dated notion now that says more about human conceit than about Your reality. We, a generation seeking Your nearness, are more apt to pray that You heal our sick than that You explain clearly to us just who You are and why You act as You do.

"I, *Adonai* your God, [am the one] who brought you out of the land of Egypt, from a slavehouse."

If You had only brought us out of the land of Egypt, *Dayenu* ("It would be sufficient for us," a recurring refrain in the Passover Haggadah's litany of God's blessings). Despite its plentiful leeks and cucumbers, its advanced culture and international status, Egypt was also where rulers were gods and idols were as much animal as human. At least the statues did not have the fallibility that made the Pharaohs' claims to divinity unbelievable, at least to the children of the children of Jacob, Leah, Rachel, Bilhah, and Zilpah. In such a country, to be created in the image of gods or to seek to imitate them could not lead to the society the Torah would envision and the Hebrews seek to establish. *Dayenu.*

Worse, Egypt was a slavehouse, literally the place where we were not free. Figuratively, it was a land where the Jewish spirit could not find itself. Literal slavery is not to be underestimated just because we no longer have enough of it in our world so that we have personal experience of slaves and slavery. The Torah, written for a world that took slavery as a human necessity, insisted that Jewish slavery must be limited to six years and extended only if the slave wished to stay with the master. Nonetheless, the Rabbis must have found even that institution sufficiently uncongenial since, while not abolishing Jewish slavery, they added severe restrictions on what the slave holder might do. It took a long time for economic reality to reflect religious idealism in this realm, but the outrage we feel when evidence comes to light of people anywhere who have, in effect, enslaved others is a testimony to what God began by bringing us out from Egypt. *Dayenu.*

But release from a slavehouse has its greatest effect on us today as a compelling metaphor for anything that releases us from any of the many bondages that impede our acting in proper freedom. The inescapable contemporary model of that exodus is what happened to our families as they went from the ghetto to emancipation. So when we now move from despotism to democracy, from ignorance to knowledge, from unemployment to a job, from discrimination to equality, from illness to health, from neurosis to maturity, from depression to hope, we know our lives have been touched by that same elemental force that so powerfully made its impact on our ex-slave forebears. And it is because God has not yet concluded all the taking out that humankind needs that we can believe that the long-ago promised days of sitting under vine and fig tree with none to make us afraid will one day come. And only when the great shofar sounds will we all be able to say the full, final, *Dayenu.*

"I, *Adonai* your God, [am the one] who brought you out of the land of Egypt, from a slavehouse. You must not..."

Ah. So that is why.

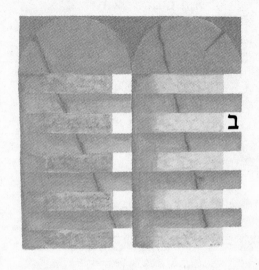

ב

two

לא יהיה לך אלהים אחרים על פני.

לא תעשה לך פסל

וכל תמונה

אשר בשמים ממעל

ואשר בארץ מתחת

ואשר במים מתחת לארץ.

לא תשתחוה להם

ולא תעבדם

כי אנכי יי אלהיך

אל קנא פקד עון

אבת על בנים

על שלשים ועל רבעים לשנאי

ועשה חסד לאלפים

לאהבי ולשמרי מצותי.

Have no other god before Me.
Let there not be to you
gods — others
on My face.
Don't make yourself a hewn statue
and any picture
of what is in heavens above
and that which is in Earth below
and that which is in the waters below the Earth.
Don't bow down to them
Don't slave for them
for I am YHVH your God
taking an account of the sins
parents inflict on the children
making their grandchildren and great-grandchildren hate Me.
I am generous to thousands
who love Me and keep my commandments.

Translation, Zalman M. Schachter-Shalomi

The Second Commandment

"Other gods"? What other gods?

General Agrippa asks Rabban Gamliel: Why should God be jealous? A warrior may be jealous of another warrior, but if the other gods are not real, why would God pay any attention to them at all? The rabbi responds with a parable: If a man takes a second wife who is superior to the first, the first wife will understand. If the second wife is inferior, the first will rightly be infuriated that her husband would lessen his devotion to her for such an unworthy woman.

A philosopher asks: Why doesn't God simply sweep the idols away? Rabban Gamliel answers: Do they worship only idols? They also worship the sun, moon, and stars. Should God destroy the entirety of creation on account of such foolishness?

Rashi teaches: Do not read "other gods" implying that there are gods other than the Lord, but read it rather as "gods of others." Or understand that they are gods who act "other" toward their worshippers, not acknowledging them in any way. These gods have no reality.

Bahya claims that these are powers such as angels or stars, which idolaters mistakenly assume are independent of God.

"On My face..."

No matter what kind of face (i.e. attitude) I display toward you, do not abandon Me. Sometimes "My face" must be angry to help you mend your ways. Do not take offense and seek to spite Me by taking a different god. *Al p'nai* can also be translated as "in My presence," which is to say in *every* time and place, it is forbidden to worship other gods. Nor can there be anyone between you and Me, as a mediator. Whatever you worship, even to get to Me, will become an idol.

"Do not make yourself a hewn statue..."

Do not make yourself into an idol. Seen in this light, we see that idolatry is far from vanquished. We consistently make our own concerns more important than God's. Even our religious

17

service can become self-serving rather than God-serving, a pick-and-choose feel-good activity that turns our own emotions into idols. We forget that the goal of worship is to give unto God, not to receive.

The Kotzker rebbe teaches: The "I" is a thief. It takes the partial and mistakes it for the whole. In our search for self-actualization and fulfillment, we seek only to achieve meaningful existence of ourselves (*yesh,* literally "there is"). True meaning lies through that fulfillment — and beyond, back toward no-thingness — to connect within the Infinite One (*ein,* literally "there is not." *Ein Sof,* "there is no end", is a mystical name for God).

How can God hold responsible the children of those who violate the command, unto third and fourth generations?

A literal translation of the verse (Exodus 20:5) might read, "visiting the guilt of the parents upon the children, upon the third and upon the fourth generations of those who reject Me..." Here, the Torah seems to contradict itself! In Deuteronomy (24:16) it teaches that parents will not die for the sins of their children or children for the sins of their parents.

One interpretation: The offspring will be punished only if the children follow in the sinful ways of their ancestors, or if it is in their power to protest but they fail to do so. It is not meant to imply that an innocent person would ever be punished. God waits, and holds back punishment so the sinner has the opportunity to repent, or so the children can do better, or so some good may yet come out of this person or family. The iniquity must be complete before any price is paid; God tells Abraham that the Canaanites cannot yet be required to give up the land because the weight of their sins is not great enough. The children of Abraham have to wait 400 years to conquer the land from the Canaanites.

Another interpretation: God takes notice of all the factors that shape a child's behavior, including the parents' actions, environmental factors, and genetic predisposition. This is God's remembrance of the parents' sins. While the children cannot escape moral responsibility for their own actions, God tempers justice with mercy by taking into account all that led to their sins. We also know that children and grandchildren often suffer the consequences of their parents' iniquity, whether it be abuse or neglect, or the inheritance of a polluted world.

The secrets within syntax

There is a singular verb *(lo yihyeh)* and a plural noun *(elohim acherim),* perhaps best translated as: "Other gods isn't for you." While this lack of agreement is not unheard of, it cries out for interpretation.

If you start worshipping any other, you will end up with all of the false gods, desperately chasing after whatever vanity you hope one of them can provide.

Another possibility: There is a singular verb so you know that the worship of even one other is forbidden. And there is a plural noun so you know that it applies to all the idols that exist or will ever be.

Is Judaism then asserting itself as the one "true" religion?

Judaism asserts that there is one true God. There is also a Divine standard, but it is always mediated by human beings. That the people will inevitably get it wrong sometimes is told in the biblical narrative itself. All religions are interpretations of God's word. While they may be able to capture some of God's will and essence, they are flawed and incomplete. Indeed, it would be idolatrous to assert any human creation is the "one true religion." Judaism simply insists on faithfulness.

A parable: A man who has to believe that his wife is the most beautiful woman in the world has no wife, for he is constantly looking at other women to be sure that none may be more beautiful. He thereby surrenders responsibility for faith in his own marriage, for sacred relationship with his life partner. You can never know whose wife (or religion) is fairest of them all, anyway, since such knowledge requires the intimacy of a life lived together (or the journey of a religious life). The purpose of religion is not to learn what is good, but to learn to do what is good, not to disclose secrets but to achieve persons. This is the discipline of living in faithfulness.

The gods we worship

Only the names change, insists Franz Rosenzwieg. It is with incomparable devotion that we serve our pantheon of today: culture, civilization, peoples, state, nation, race, art, science, economy, and class. This is certainly an abbreviated and incomplete list of our contemporary gods. And there are consequences to our idolatry, as Ralph Waldo Emerson warns:

> The gods we worship write their names on our faces, be sure of that. And we will worship something — have no doubt of that either. We may think that our tribute is paid in secret in the dark recesses of the heart — but it will out. That which dominates our imagination and our thoughts will determine our life and character. Therefore it behooves us to be careful what we are worshipping, for what we are worshipping we are becoming.

— *Rachel S. Mikva*

No Other

ZALMAN M. SCHACTER-SHALOMI

I was still a card-carrying Lubavitcher, though not that "fundamentalist" anymore. I did not get too easily to the place where I could see Conservative and Reform rabbis as real colleagues. Where I first started after my ordination was in a place where all religious non-Jews were idolaters and non-Orthodox Jews were heretics. The true spiritual treasures were among the Jews, and even among Jews mostly with the Chasidim, and even among the Chasidim mostly with the Lubavitchers whose rebbes demanded that they do the inner work of *davenen* (prayer) at length and meditate on Chasidic teaching. In those years I still concentrated all my efforts on trying to restore traditional halachic Judaism (in accordance with Jewish law) in America and the world. I knew that it could not come by persuading people to adopt outward observance. We had to meet the spiritual needs of people.

Having been trained in Chabad Chasidism with its emphasis on *hitbonenut* (interior prayer and contemplative meditation), I felt a missionary's drive to share these spiritual treasures with any Jew who would be interested. People who worked with youth — Hillel, Ramah, Olin-Sang-Ruby Union Institute, Brandeis-Bardin Camp Institute — invited me, as did all sorts of non-Orthodox congregations, and I sought to share with them in the hope that once we offered people some real spiritual nourishment from our traditional treasure house, we would be able to persuade them to live "Torah True" lives. I still stood on the halachic chessboard and it was limited to the sixty-four squares within the four cubits of the halachah, with the move of each piece on it determined by their role and rule. There is a cryptic statement in the Talmud: "Since the day that the Temple was destroyed, the Holy One of Blessing has nothing in this world but the four cubits of halachah alone." While it can be interpreted in several ways, all surely indicate that the substance and process of Jewish law were considered the remaining guides for Jewish life.

Wisdom among the nations — believe it. Torah among the nations — don't believe it. What does the *midrash* (Jewish textual interpretation) say about those who adhered to other religions? They were right, only inasmuch as their religions encouraged them to observe the seven Noahide commandments. (Jewish tradition holds that seven laws were given to all people during the time of Noah: Establish courts of justice, do not eat meat cut from a living animal, and do not engage in idolatry, adultery, blasphemy, murder, or robbery.) Several sources suggest that they also had a residue left with them from the time when God, walking around with the Torah, asked the other nations if they wanted to accept the Torah and, after they looked at it, they refused. But they looked, didn't they? And from that look came the kernel of truth of their religion. All but that kernel was — if not *avodat elilim* (the worship of idols) — then at best it was for Jews off limits as *avodah zarah* (foreign worship).

Imagine the surprise when I, then teaching at a Lubavitcher yeshivah, discovered some books that taught me that "idolaters" were also *ma'aminim,* real believers in the living God, and that Trappists also did "mental prayer" and that Hindus had rebbes like Ramakrishna. This — and later the challenge I received from Howard Thurman, dean of the chapel of Boston University, my black rebbe: "Zalman! Don't you trust the *Ruach Hakodesh* [the Holy Spirit]?" — threw me into turmoil. As Reb Mosheh Pekarsky taught me, "*Moshe kibeil torah misinai.* Moses received [a] Torah at Sinai." "A" Torah, not "the" Torah.

I believed — and still believe — in the workings of Divine Providence as Chasidism taught it: *hashgachah peratit,* specific Divine Providence that ordains even how a leaf falls. And so I had to face a Providence that produced a Buddha, a LaoTzu, great souls no less than our rebbes. Were they an accidental oops of God? And what about the Nazarene Chasidim who followed their rebbe Jesus? Did not the Chasidim of Reb Nachman of Bratzlav believe in a rebbe who no longer lived on Earth?

My restoration theology started to break down and it began to reorganize itself on another level. Much happened to me in those years. I met people like Thomas Merton, Howard Thurman, Timothy Leary and Richard Alpert, Zen Roshis, Swamis, nuns and priests, ministers and transpersonal therapists. I went to Esalen and Berkeley, finding New Age ideas and experiences; I lived through a sexual revolution, divorces, and marriages. All of these had a bearing on my emerging reality map. Auschwitz, Hiroshima, the moon walk, feminism and ecology, the hole in the ozone layer, and the emergence of Gaia (Earth alive and aware) — all of these made me take another look at our tradition.

Continuing and participating in the evolving process of our Torah, I saw that I had changed from someone who had advocated restoration to one who now espoused renewal — an ongoing process of staying at the growing edge of the Tree of Life (a metaphor for Torah, all of sacred learning), both juicy and in touch with the environment. I no longer saw the world in sectarian-ideological terms.

I still believe that we must not practice idolatry. We must obey this crucial command, albeit with a current reading that does not denigrate other religions, a reading that is in accord with an organismic perspective. Still, I want to affirm that the earlier readings of this commandment were not only necessary but also right considering the zeitgeist of the peoples who surrounded us. We needed a high degree of surface tension that would keep us separate so that we could keep serving our purpose, just as the heart needs to be a heart and the liver needs to be a liver. We cannot put a living organism through a blender, homogenize it, and expect it to stay alive.

So my thesis is now, after the paradigm shift I experienced, that the second commandment means: Real idolatry today is the worship of money, technology, addictions, absolute political systems — even of "Judaism" and of the personal ego. None of the religions of other peoples is *avodat elilim*. Even a-theistic Buddhism can make sense to someone who knows of the Holy No-Thing, the *ayin* of *Ein Sof* (literally, the no-thingness of God, the One without end). In Jewish mysticism, we attempt to transcend self-awareness in order to cling to God's infinite Being. I honor them all and will ask other Jews to honor them as God's ways to communicate with people. But, as religions, they are for Jews *avodah zarah* — a strange worship, incompatible with our immune system. Their spiritual tools, though, can be and are helpful to Jews who find them helpful in keeping their allegiance to our faith and people.

I have been initiated into being an organismic braincell of the global brain, a Gaian who is a Jew. As one who affirms Earth as a living organism, *Melech ha'olam* (King of the Universe) now has a meaning grounded in my perception of concrete holistic reality. But as a Jew, it still makes a claim on me for absolute faithfulness and primacy. Complete faith is not a simple thing. All the other powers in the world cry out for us to make them more important than God, to idolize them. We must not turn our products, ourselves, or even our goals into gods.

The story is told how a Chasid asked Reb Mosheh of Kobrin for help because he could not say the *Ani Ma'amin* (a prayer of God's attributes named for its first words, "I believe"). If he really believed with perfect faith as this set of 13 Principles of Faith articulated by Maimonides insisted, he would be a different person. So the rebbe asked him, "What if you did not say the *Ani Ma'amin?*" The Chasid answered, "Then how could I call myself a Jew?" So they agreed that from now on the Chasid would say, "*Halevai she'ani ma'amin* — Would that I believed," and the credo became a prayerful aspiration.

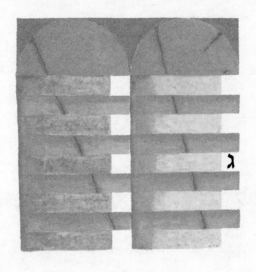

three

לא תשא

את שם יי אלהיך

לשוא

כי לא ינקה יי

את אשר ישא את שמו לשוא.

You shall not lift up
the name of *Adonai* your God
for vain purpose,
for *Adonai* will not clear
one who uses the Name in vain.

The Third Commandment

"For vain purpose..."

Jewish tradition distinguishes two types of vanity: using God's name unnecessarily (as in swearing to the completely obvious), and using God's name falsely. The latter may include swearing to contradict known facts, to deceive, or to do what you clearly lack the means or strength to do. The Essenes taught that one who cannot be believed without swearing is already condemned.

The Talmud extends the prohibition to using God's name in any superfluous way, not simply in oaths. As Nachmanides later points out, it does not say here that you must not swear in God's name for vain purpose, but that you must not "lift it up" at all for vanity. Thus, even an unnecessary or unfulfilled blessing (such as saying kiddush, but not drinking the wine) violates the command. In our society, where God's name is often used without even realizing it, superfluity seems to be the rule rather than the exception.

Using God's name for an unworthy purpose (say for magic or for destructive goals) is especially serious. Nonetheless, human history is replete with examples of humanity lifting up the name of God for its own evil purposes.

How far do we take it?

If you commit to an action, but do not keep your word — even if you do not invoke the name of God — is it possible to violate this commandment? If you identify yourself as a religious person, and then demonstrate that you are untrustworthy (or brutal or stingy or...), have you not sullied the reputation of God? After all, what is a name?

Remember Moses, who was kept from the Land of Promise simply because he failed once to sanctify God's name in front of the people. If we are religious people, is everything we say and do somehow a reflection on God's name? This consciousness is part of the ethical discipline of a truly religious life.

We are cautioned not to "carry God's name upon ourselves." If we set ourselves up as God's representative and we are not worthy, we have violated this command.

Who are we to speak of God at all?

Rabbi Joseph Soloveitchik teaches that it is a presumption for us to believe any language can avoid misrepresenting God or misusing the name for our own purposes. It is a paradox for dust and ashes to address a transcendent being at all. This utterance, then, is gracious permission to use the Name, a kindness bestowed upon us by the One who knows how much we need to connect God to our lives. But it has boundaries.

The kaddish prayer can be seen as a creation of this ethic. Not originally a mourner's prayer at all, it initially served as a caveat at the end of a study session and then after a section of the worship service. A key phrase is the acknowledgment that God is to be praised, glorified, exalted, honored — there are four more synonyms — even though God is beyond all the praises, songs, and adorations that we can utter. There is no way that our finite minds can understand the fullness of God, much less articulate it, yet we cannot desist from the search for connection and comprehension.

The Name

Jewish tradition attempts to draw a fence around this command by discouraging oaths altogether, and by limiting the articulation of the actual Hebrew name for God. Only the High Priest on Yom Kippur was allowed to say it. As he uttered it inside the Holy of Holies in the Temple in Jerusalem, the people fell on their faces. With the destruction of the Temple, this ritual came to an end and the pronunciation of the name became lost. Some Christian groups have attempted to reconstruct it as Jehovah, some scholars suggest Yahweh, but most Jews decline to seek it out.

So we say *Adonai,* which means "my Lord," or *Hashem,* meaning "the Name." Still, even a "nickname" for God must be used with care.

When written down, any direct name (*Elohim,* God; *Adonai,* Lord) is never to be erased or discarded, according to Jewish tradition, lest that be another form of vanity. Many people, therefore, leave out a letter, insert a dash, or substitute a letter in the Hebrew if the text is not to be used for permanent, sacred purpose. Anything with God's name upon it, according to Jewish law, is to be stored or buried in a *genizah* (consecrated earth or vault) when it can no longer serve its sacred purpose. This practice has enabled us to rediscover many ancient texts, such as the outstanding historical finds at the Cairo *genizah*.

"For *Adonai* will not clear one who uses the Name in vain..."

What sort of penalty is this? Only this utterance and the one against idolatry mention a punishment. Why? Because taking God's name in vain often escapes the notice of humanity (and, in some cases, may be beyond our power to judge). You may think you are off the hook, but here is a Judge you cannot deceive, and Who believes that what you say matters.

We will fall short

Judaism takes very seriously the power of words. How strange, then, that a central prayer of the Yom Kippur liturgy, *Kol Nidrei,* nullifies our oaths. Since God is often invoked in these vows, is this not taking the Name in vain?

Although the prayer is commonly associated with Marranos in fifteenth-century Spain who felt compelled to convert to Christianity but secretly practiced Judaism, it is much older, going back to the ninth century. Through the years, rabbis objected to the legalistic invalidation of our oaths and tried to eliminate the prayer, but popular opinion would not let it go. The music associated with it in the Ashkenazi world is a strong element in that attachment, but so is the concept that we will inevitably speak words in vain. *Kol Nidrei* becomes emblematic of the entire exercise of repentance. It is because of the gravity of our words that some release is needed, a way to start over. We cannot change our ways until we find forgiveness for the sins and vanities of our past, and even though we know we will fall short again, our commitments are sincere, our atonement real.

— *Rachel S. Mikva*

Thou Shalt Not Take the Name

NANCY FUCHS-KREIMER

> On the day when the angels came to testify
> before the Lord, the Accusing Angel came too.
> The Accuser said, "Just reach out and strike
> [Job's] flesh and bones, and I bet he'll curse you
> to your face."
>
> The Lord said, "All right. He is in your power."

Despite popular impression, the Book of Job does not focus on the question: Why do the righteous suffer? The very beginning of the book disposes of that issue. Job suffers because the Accuser made a bet with God. The Book of Job is about a different query: How shall we talk about God in the midst of a suffering world? How shall we talk to God? What does it mean to take the name of the Lord in vain, and what would it mean to lift up the name of the Lord correctly? I, too, have wondered about the meaning of the third commandment. I have wrestled with that question in dialogue with Jewish tradition, with the Book of Job, and with the unfolding story of my life.

• • •

"God damn!" I blurted out. I was a ten-year-old reaching for words to express my indignation at having stubbed my toe. It was just a phrase I had heard, something to say when angry. My mother, rewinding a rusty tape recorder in her brain, pushed PLAY: "Thou shalt not take the name of thy Lord in vain." I was dumbfounded. Everyday I was admonished to be kind, to share with my brother and sister, to tell the truth. These were presented as the right things to do. The "Lord" was never brought into the discussion. Come to think of it, God was not mentioned at all, for any reason. My mother seemed less concerned about this rule than about kindness and truth-telling. No wonder she resorted to the archaic language of the Bible. This was a rule that made no sense except in context. (If there is no God, what does it matter how we use "His" name?)

Actually, this had very little to do with God. It was about being proper and appropriate, not rude and out of line. But mostly it was about getting angry. What was bad about cursing, I concluded, was that it shows you are angry, which you should not be. When you are angry, keep it to yourself. Better still, don't become angry at all. But in the meantime, I was intrigued. Who is this "Lord" and why did it matter so much to people how "His" name was used?

• • •

> Now Job had three friends — Eliphaz the Temanite, Bildad the Shuhite, and Zopher the Namathite. When these friends heard of all the calamities that had come upon him, each of them left his own country to mourn with Job and to comfort him.

I was thirteen, blessedly untouched by death, attending my first funeral. Great Uncle Al left his shocked and terrified widow, and two children not much older than I. This was something new to me. But even newer was the theology of the free-lance rabbi hired by the funeral home for the occasion. He provided a clumsy compendium of "it's all for the best," promises of the afterlife, and "it could have been worse." (From the rabbi's point of view, that last statement was strictly true; it could have happened to him.)

I was devastated. Not by the death, but by the rabbi. Such *vain* comfort. How dare this rabbi bring God into all this sadness and in such a patently unbelievable fashion? I had come to the conclusion that God is the sum of all that is good and wondrous in the world; now God's name was being misused for what I believed to be false consolation. This, I concluded, is what it means to take God's name in vain. Oblivious to the fact that at the time there were no rabbinical schools that accepted women, I decided then and there to become a rabbi.

• • •

When I entered rabbinical school, they should have asked for my passport at the door. In order to become a rabbi, I had to first immigrate and acculturate to a new world: Judaism. In addition to a foreign language or two, I also discovered customs and patterns of thought that were foreign to me. At the end of my first year, I went to lunch at someone's home for the second day of Shavuot. The hostess served raspberries, explaining that since this was the first time this season that the family had eaten raspberries it was OK to say a *shehecheyanu* (a prayer that blesses God for giving us life, for sustaining us, and for helping us reach a moment of new blessing). On the second day of a festival, one is tempted to recite this blessing, but without a new reason for saying it — such as it being the first day of a holiday or eating the first raspberries of the season — it would be a *berachah levatalah,* a blessing uttered in vain.

This confused me. I had recently learned that Judaism was insistent on blessing everything imaginable, that the Talmud suggests we utter one hundred blessings each day. At the time, this seemed excessive but compelling in its jubilant extravagance. It never occurred to me you could overdo it. Now, I learned that despite this seeming enthusiasm for blessing, there was also a danger of blessing when one isn't supposed to bless and that this misdeed had a name: *berachah levatalah.* Words are abundant in our world; people are constantly talking. So what's a blessing or two among friends? I looked up the origin of the rule in the Talmud. It all goes back to that third commandment; to the rabbis, an extraneous blessing is taking the name of the Lord in vain.

Shortly after that lunch, I studied a passage in the Talmud that was almost as hard for me to understand in English as it was in Aramaic. The Rabbis recollect that Moses, on one occasion, referred to the "great, mighty and awesome God." But, they also recall, Jeremiah described God as just "great and mighty." The rabbis conclude from this that Jeremiah must not have found God awesome. Daniel also changed the wording of Moses. Apparently

Daniel did not believe that God was mighty — else why would strangers be enslaving his children? — so he called God simply "great and awesome."

How, then, should a Jew pray? The Great Assembly (the religious authority for the Jewish community in the Persian empire, possibly third–fourth century BCE) chose to restore to God the full Mosaic description. On what grounds? They believed that God's might and awesomeness were indeed in evidence in God's patience with evildoers and the fact that the people of Israel survives. But it does not end there. The Rabbis also expressed their support for Jeremiah and Daniel in their insistence on being true to their own experience. As Rabbi Eliezer said, "They would not lie to the Holy One."

What could it possibly mean to *lie* to the Holy One? As if the Holy One wouldn't know? At first blush, taking God's name in vain appears to be a crime without human victims, and indeed, commentators note that it is for this reason that only the third commandment specifies that God will not forgive you. Presumably, in the case of the other commandments there will be humans who will be eager to bring you to justice. If you say God's name unnecessarily in a prayer or if you use God's name when not in prayer, *who cares?* Jewish tradition cares enough to substitute *Elokim* or *Hashem* for God's name in conversation (changing the name slightly so as not to really use it). What is it to God if we eat strawberries or raspberries, or throw in an extra adjective or two when praising? God, Who is above such matters, shouldn't be troubled. But clearly, words matter — and words about God matter a lot.

The rabbinate led me to a career in writing and teaching about theology. When it came to the third commandment, this was an extremely high-risk profession. I wondered: Was I using the name of God extraneously? I chose to call my flimsy intuitions of meaning, my glimpses of transcendence, my hopes for holiness: *God.* Could I call my mishmash of faith and doubt and spiritual longings the same thing my great-grandmother called her Creator?

I reread the third commandment in context. The first commandment states the premise: "I am the Lord Your God." The next two commandments offer two polar opposite ways of violating that premise. First, we go astray by having other gods or by making an image of the one God, making God so concrete and so rigid in concept as to be no longer God but an idol. Now *there* is a sermon I love to preach: If you say God must be "He," if you know God's gender, have you not chiseled God in stone for all time and made a graven image of the imageless God? Isn't it violating the second commandment to utter traditional prayers in such a rote and boring way as to leave them, as the Chasidic story goes, lying heavy like dead leaves around the synagogue floor? The words have become the idol; God has ceased to be alive within them. So much for the Scylla. The third commandment points to the Charybdis. If God can be anyone or anything, God becomes no thing, triviality, vanity. The name of God is lifted up for naught when God, rather than being set in stone, becomes so amorphous a being as to fit whatever one feels good about. In the New Age writings I enjoyed, God, far from being too concrete, was freelance and generic. By joining the ranks of popular spirituality writers, was I promoting a God without the rules, the hard questions, and the bite? By too easily claiming and naming God, by encouraging others to do the same, did I take the name of the Lord in vain?

I started teaching rabbinical students about Freud. Whatever his failings, Freud did not break the third commandment. Better not to lift up the name of God at all than to take it and make mush. Freud taught us: Evil is indeed real and it is right inside us (the very place I most often looked for God!). He then said that to draw upon God as consolation for our miseries is to misuse the name. People often assume that Freud was critical of orthodox religion. But, in fact, Freud's critique is also aimed very tellingly at the liberals. If you don't really believe, don't say you do. Don't distort the name.

If we don't take seriously the existence of evil, the potential of humans for sinfulness and error, the radically awful stuff in the universe, we turn God's name into triviality. But how to reconcile God with evil? How do we bless God for the evil even as we bless God for the good? That is the question at the heart of observing the third commandment. If we don't probe with some intellectual honesty our own experience that God sometimes (often) seems neither awesome nor great (and the Great Assembly's verbal gymnastics do not suffice), then we are not being honest to God. We are making God's name a breath, an emptiness. If we haven't thought this through and felt it through, no amount of raspberries will help; all our blessings will be in vain.

• • •

And now I am in agony;
the days of sorrow have caught me.
Pain pierces my skin;
suffering gnaws my bones.

Our friend, a mother of four young children, discovered she had cancer. For two and a half years, not a Sabbath went by that we did not say a *mi sheberach,* a prayer that seeks healing of body and spirit for her. We understood these blessings to be calls to ourselves to become the community that would be God's presence. So we organized and we networked. Scores of people gave blood, made visits, drove carpools, delivered casseroles. We joked that our spiritual practice was talking on the phone. It seemed to us that God (the process that makes for good in the universe) could indeed heal the sick.

On an intellectual level, I knew that prayers could not affect the objective outcome of the disease. It was bad theology, even in Orthodoxy, to expect that it would. (The tradition says that if you pray for a boy after becoming pregnant, you are taking God's name in vain since the gender is already established.) Yet on an emotional level, all the talk of "healing and Judaism" had me convinced otherwise. Saying all those blessings brought me back to the world of magical thinking, to the notion that I could somehow influence the universe to go my way.

Some scholars believe that it is precisely this error that was at the heart of the third commandment. Don't lift up God's name for manipulation like the pagans do. It is in vain, says the commandment. It simply will not work. Our friend died. *As the fishes that are taken in an evil net...so are the daughters of men snared in an evil time...."* (Ecclesiastes 9:12).

• • •

> I am speechless: what can I answer?
> I put my hand on my mouth
> I have said too much already;
> Now I will speak no more....
> I had heard of you with my ears,
> But now my eyes have seen you
> Therefore will I be quiet, comforted that I am dust.

A Jewish foundation thought the world would be a better place if once a year fifteen rabbis said nothing for three days. As soon as I heard about this opportunity to participate in a silent Buddhist retreat, I knew that I would attend. I had never sat in meditation. (I had rarely sat still.) But this sounded like an appealing prospect. One cannot take the Name in vain if one says nothing about the Name, or anything else for that matter.

After my first two days in silence, I went to the spiritual advisor for my five-minute consultation. I told her that after years of struggling with traditional Jewish prayer, all this silence had left me with an overwhelming desire to talk to God. Not about God. *To* God. She gave me special dispensation to speak — aloud — but only to God, and only if I went far off away from the group. The next time there was a "walking meditation," I headed for the woods. And there, alone, I poured out my heart to God. All my fears, all my sorrows, all my junk. I discovered a considerable amount of anger. And it didn't feel like I was taking the name of the Lord in vain. If I wanted to avoid lying to the Holy One, if I wanted to be "honest to God," I had *better* be allowed to be angry.

• • •

> God damn the day I was born and the night that
> forced me from the womb.

This sentence, uttered by Job as his opening volley, might well qualify as the most blasphemous statement in the Bible: cursing God by cursing God's greatest gift — life. One thing is clear. This is a statement of anger, and a statement of acknowledgment: God is about evil. So, we acknowledge — first in anger and then, if we are graced to sit with it long enough, perhaps in another key.

37

The Talmud says that a person is known by his pocket, his cup, and his rage. Perhaps if we can be with our rage, we can see it form itself anew as a serenity of sorts and we will emerge more compassionate and more generous. Perhaps we will even be able to laugh again. Recall the *midrash* written by shocked and sorrowing Jews after their defeat by the Romans. What were they to do with the verse, "Who is like You among the gods (אלים, *elim*)?" One rabbi suggested slightly reworking it to read, "Who is like You among the mute (אלמים, *ilemim*)?" That, at least, was frank. Resigned, but still feisty. A person is known by his humor as well as by his anger.

A friend of mine visited her mother, who is a Holocaust survivor and an Orthodox Jew. Sitting in the park together, they heard one of her mother's friends talking. "What a beautiful wedding I went to last night. The *chassen* (groom) was a *mensch,* a gentle young man, so sweet and for once he wasn't sleeping." My friend could not understand why the *chassen* would be sleeping, but the woman clarified her words. She was not referring to the groom but to God: "*Er shluft a sach,* He sleeps a lot." This observant Jewish woman knew what God was supposed to do. She also knew what she knew about life. She refused to gloss over her own truth, so she told a story that makes sense to her of the way things seem to go. There is a great, mighty and awesome God ruling the universe but He sleeps a lot. The psalmist asked, "Why do You sleep?" (Psalm 44:24). She was not bothering to ask that question anymore, but she was prepared to bless the moments when, against all odds, joy seemed to be breaking through.

• • •

> The Lord said to Eliphaz the Temanite, "I am very
> angry at you and your two friends, because you
> have not spoken the truth about me as my ser-
> vant Job has.... My servant Job will pray for you
> and for his sake I will overlook your sin."

In the end, God seems to appreciate his apologists very little. God does, however, appear to value honesty.

As for the third commandment, we must lift up God's name for fullness. We must speak about God, and speak to God. And be sure to do more of the latter than the former. We must speak from the depths of our experience, of our feelings, of our hearts and acknowledge it all: the God who, like a doting grandparent, treasures our every gesture and the one who, as Shakespeare noticed, like a wanton boy with flies, kills us for sport.

Say it all out loud. Care about getting it right. Hold on to all your joy — and to all your hurt. Ignore mealy-mouthed defenses of God that leave you taking the blame. Avoid people who have anything too quick and pious to say about God. Pray you can reach a place where the good and the evil can be heard in stereo and the music will sound sweet. In anticipation of that day of unity, just for practice, raise up the name of God in praise. For those blessed raspberries whose taste is truly a miracle to be savored. For those microseconds that "He opens His eyes from His slumber" and lets "His" glory shine. Place your bet on God's goodness. Go to lots of weddings. Sing. Dance. Like the woman of valor, "laugh until your very last day." When in doubt, recall the line from psalms with which Maimonides ended his own lengthy theological reflections, "*Lecha tehilah dumiah*. To You, silence is praise."

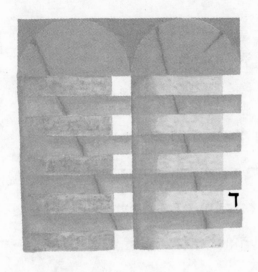

four

זכור את יום השבת לקדשו.

ששת ימים תעבד

ועשית כל מלאכתך.

ויום השביעי שבת ליי אלהיך

לא תעשה כל מלאכה

אתה ובנך ובתך עבדך ואמתך

ובהמתך וגרך אשר בשעריך.

כי ששת ימים עשה יי

את השמים ואת הארץ

את הים ואת כל אשר בם

וינח ביום השביעי

על כן ברך יי

את יום השבת ויקדשהו.

Remember the Sabbath day and keep it holy.
Six days you shall labor
and do all of your work.
But the seventh day is a Sabbath of the Lord your God
you shall not do any work
you, your son or daughter, your male or female slave,
or your cattle, or the stranger who is within your settlements.
For in six days the Lord made
heaven and earth
and sea, and all that is in them,
and He rested on the seventh day
therefore the Lord blessed
the Sabbath day and hallowed it.

The Fourth Commandment

All your work?

"Six days you shall labor and do all of your work...." But it is impossible to accomplish all our work in six days! The gift of the Sabbath is the command to rest *as if* all of our work is done. Suddenly, then, there is time to pray, study, meditate, take a long walk, sing, celebrate with awe and appreciation, rediscover family and friends, rediscover ourselves.

A palace in time

Notice that the first thing God consecrates in this world is not a thing or a place, but a moment in time. As Abraham Joshua Heschel writes:

> Technical civilization is man's conquest of space.
> It is a triumph frequently achieved by sacrificing
> an essential ingredient of existence, namely,
> time. In technical civilization, we expend time to
> gain space.... The meaning of the Sabbath is to
> celebrate time rather than space. Six days a
> week we live under the tyranny of things of
> space; on the Sabbath we try to become attuned
> to holiness in time. It is a day on which we are
> called upon to share in what is eternal in time,
> to turn from the results of creation to the mys-
> tery of creation; from the world of creation to the
> creation of the world.

A taste of the World to Come

If you want to experience something of the spiritual existence of the World to Come, sanctify the Shabbat. Because the tradition affirms that this day is, indeed, a foretaste of the world already redeemed, daily prayers seeking the Divine grace that leads up to it — knowledge, forgiveness, health, abundance, freedom, justice, etc. — are removed from the worship service. The world is already whole, if only for a day.

At the end of Shabbat we sing to Elijah, herald of the messianic age. Soon, we pray, will be the Sabbath that never ends.

"Keep" and "Remember" in a single utterance

The text of the Ten Commandments as it appears in Exodus is not identical to the text as it appears in Deuteronomy. Among the distinctions is a different verb for our honoring the Sabbath: "*Zachor,* Remember" is replaced by "*Shamor,* Keep." Does Moses have the chutzpah to change God's word in his repetition of these commanding utterances? No, say the Rabbis. Rather, they are both articulated by God in the one singular revelation. But why are they both necessary?

The Talmud teaches that *zachor* reminds us to celebrate the positive, such as fine food and Torah study, and *shamor* charges us to guard against violating the "do not's". The spirit of Shabbat is lost if we take from it only a series of restrictions and forget to rejoice. It is also lost if we fail to see the holiness of committing to certain limits.

How does God make the Sabbath holy?

Ibn Ezra: Our ability to absorb wisdom and insight is heightened on this day.

Ramban: It draws its holiness from higher spheres of existence.

Or Hachayim: God raises it above the vicissitudes of this world.

How do we make the Sabbath holy?

To sanctify Shabbat must be more than guarding against technical violations of the Sabbath, and more than thoughtlessly performing a few rituals. To sanctify the Sabbath, we must make it the essence of our being, the soul of our time. We seek in each moment to draw closer to God, and discover the powerful spirit of the day. Then we will know the true celebration of holiness. There is no greater thrill.

If you refrain from trampling the Sabbath, from
pursuing your affairs on My holy day;

If you call the Sabbath "delight", *Adonai's* holy
day "honored";

And you honor it, without doing what you
always do; not pursuing your business, nor even
speaking of it;

Then you shall delight yourself in *Adonai*.

(Isaiah 58:13–14)

Ma'aseh shehayah... It once happened

that a man was strolling through his vineyard on the Sabbath,
and noticed a breach in the wall around his property. His immediate thought was to repair it after the Sabbath ended, but then
felt he had profaned the holy day by planning his weekday
work activity. The man resolved never to repair that breach in
the wall. Moved by his devotion, the Holy One of Blessing
caused a huge fruit tree to grow in the gap, mending the wall
and yielding the beautiful blessing of fruit.

One who gives of himself to the Sabbath, the Sabbath will
repay.

Shabbat as protest

Western civilization, especially in its contemporary form,
detests things that are inefficient. The Roman philosopher
Seneca taught that spending every seventh day without "doing
anything" wastes one seventh of your life. Against that comes
the teaching that not all value can be measured in physical
productivity. Rabbi Gunther Plaut teaches, "We must understand that doing nothing, being silent and open to the world,
letting things happen inside, can be as important as — and
sometimes more important than — what we commonly call
'useful.'" The Sabbath is the ultimate statement that the world
does not own us.

The pause between the notes

A great pianist was once asked by an ardent admirer: "How do you handle the notes as well as you do?" The artist answered: "The notes I handle no better than many pianists, but the pauses between the notes — ah! that is where the art resides."

In great living, as in great music, the art may be in the pauses. Surely one of the enduring contributions that Judaism made to the art of living was Shabbat, "the pause between the notes." And it is to Shabbat that we must look if we are to restore to our lives the sense of serenity and sanctity that Shabbat offers in such joyous abundance.

Shabbat was last in creation but first in intention. It was not created for the sake of the other days; rather the other days were created for the sake of Shabbat. It is not an interlude, but a climax.

At the center of Jewish life

Ahad HaAm reminds us: A Jew who feels a real tie to the life of our people throughout the generations will find it utterly impossible to think of the existence of the Jew without Shabbat. One can say without exaggeration that more than the people of Israel have kept Shabbat, Shabbat has kept the people of Israel.

— Rachel S. Mikva

The Meaning of Shabbat: A Virtual Domain in Time

Lawrence A. Hoffman

To the chagrin of some people, observing the Sabbath appears in the Ten Commandments not simply as a universally good idea (a day of rest each week — who can argue with that?), but as a specifically commanded Jewish thing to do. How do Wall Street traders, cosmopolitan travelers, and skeptical sophisticates of other varieties make sense of keeping Shabbat as a *mitzvah* that has nothing to do with "rest and relaxation"? We all concede the need to be good, ethical, even God-fearing (though we dislike the word "fear"). But ritually observant with regard to Shabbat? Shabbat legislation ought to marked with an asterisk, we imagine, as if the Torah had said, "Here are nine commandments — and a suggestion."

On the scale of significance, we put ritual somewhere lower than ethics but higher than food preferences. Traditional Jewish communities, however, would not see it that way because, for them, ritual carries the same Divine authority as do the ethical *mitzvot*. The rest of us worry little about God's censure for mere ritual breaches, and we know we will not even face social and economic ostracism for violating Shabbat. Our problem is that our world view has come to preclude the once-popular notion that we do God's will to attain reward or to ward off punishment.

The rhetoric of limits: Shabbat as a calculus of reward and punishment

The doctrine of reward and punishment goes back to the Rabbis and is typified by a rhetoric of limits. It derives from the rabbinic map of reality, which saw the world as a vast, invisible maze, where people must find their way from birth to death without bumping into the walls. The classic texts of rabbinic literature — Talmud,

47

codes, and legal commentaries — constitute "a way of walking," which is the literal meaning of the Hebrew term *halachah,* usually understood as "Jewish law." The Rabbis give us a continually upgraded guide book through the maze, telling us to turn left, not right; eat this way, not that; wear these clothes, not those. The universe consists not of what is, but of what human beings may or may not do with what is.

Not that rabbinic Judaism is dry legalism. It is far from that. It exudes spirituality, beauty, meaning, and love, not just rules, even if the rules are paramount. Indeed, one of the rules for the Sabbath is to rejoice in it (see Isaiah 58:13). But limits predominate, and God is the primary enforcer of the limits.

The traditional liturgy suggests God's role by likening Shabbat to a divine gift. Every Friday night the Sabbath is inaugurated with the sentence, "God gave us His [sic] holy Sabbath as an inheritance." Another Sabbath prayer pleads with God to continue giving us this Sabbath as our righteous bequest. The first instance teaches us that Israel received the Sabbath originally as a gift of God's grace. The second case characterizes this gift as contingent; it has strings attached. It may be taken back if we prove unworthy. The fear of being unworthy is endemic to limit thinking, which envisions humans as standing before God like children before a parent, who gives or takes, rewards or punishes. So God gives, but we must live up to the gifts. Good boys and girls take care of their things. Good Jews take care of the Sabbath.

Fear of punishment and hope of reward were never foolproof motivation. The command to keep Shabbat had scarcely been given when an Israelite in the wilderness decided to collect wood on the seventh day instead of resting (Numbers, Chapter 15). He quickly discovered, however, that when failure to look after what we are given has consequences, the limits become persuasive: The stick-gatherer was stoned to death, and there are no more tales of Sabbath violations in the wilderness. Similar cases can be drawn from almost any point in history: In seventeenth- and eighteenth-century Salonika, for instance, almost every Jew attended coffee houses on Shabbat to drink coffee that had been prepared that day for the express needs of the Jewish patrons. Rabbis inveighed in vain against this patent breach of Jewish law. A drought finally convinced them that God was indeed punishing them, and (temporarily, at least) they abstained from the coffee houses. When rain finally fell, however, and normality reigned again, people returned to their old habit. The Rabbis continued to preach the lesson of limits, but after the sermon, their congregants went out for coffee as usual.

We no longer believe that droughts in Salonika (or anywhere else) have anything to do with the Sabbath. Even in eighteenth-century Salonika, people were already feeling the faint winds of the Enlightenment, bringing news of modern science and a universe that operated with certain and dependable truths, not divine whim. Nineteenth-century Jews therefore abandoned the rhetoric of limits and reinterpreted the Sabbath as a truth in its own right, or (using the language of German idealism) an idea, namely, the idea of human sanctity.

The rhetoric of truth: Shabbat as divine truth

Religion, too, has truths to tell. Unable to imagine God primarily as a rewarding and punishing keeper of limits, modern theologians revamped God's image. The 1885 Pittsburgh Platform of American Reform Judaism summed it up by calling God "the God idea"; God became the central religious truth of the human race.

Germany's enlightened Jews flocked to temples not so much to pray, and certainly not because they felt they had to go (that would have been limit thinking), but to hear spiritual truths from rabbis who had attended college, who were addressed as "Doctor," and who claimed expertise in "the science [!] of Judaism." The duration of the prayer service shrank, as old-time prayers were shortened or jettisoned because they were either irrelevant or "untruthful." But a new slot in the service was invented and expanded: the sermon, which was the truth-telling spot in the program.

If we turn now to the Sabbath, we find a radical statement of the Sabbath's essence by the German Reform rabbis:

> The Sabbath is a day of consecration which is
> sanctified through our sanctifying ourselves; a
> day the distinctiveness of which is to be brought
> forcibly home to us by our ceasing from our daily

toil and our daily tasks, and giving ourselves to
contemplation of the divine purpose of our existence as indicated by Jewish teaching. Hence, no
task should be forbidden which conduces toward
recreation and spiritual elevation.

How deftly they move from "is" to "ought," from the truth of the
Sabbath idea to the guidelines for Sabbath practice. There are still
Sabbath limits here, but truth comes first. Limits flow from truths.
Jews may keep the Sabbath because its observance is consistent
with the Sabbath as a day of sanctification, not because of the
limit-thinking calculus of divine reward and punishment.

Imbued with a scientific claim to certainty, the great Reform
rabbis of the modern era assumed that historical truths would, in
and of themselves, clarify their inherited rabbinic limits. If they
could discover where Shabbat came from, they would know how
much of it to keep. If, that is, Shabbat were found to be historically
derived from the Babylonian festival *Shabbatu,* they could separate
"foreign" Babylonian influence from "authentic" Jewish teaching,
and dispense with the former while keeping the latter. Limits
would emerge through truth. The truths of the physical universe
were for science to discover; religion specialized in truths of the
spirit. The Sabbath became a spiritual truth that the physical sciences would never arrive at: the idea of sanctifying humanity.

Prayers in early Reform liturgies reflect truth-thinking. The
first official edition of the Reform movement's *Union Prayer Book*
revised the prayer known as *Kedushat Hayom* ("Sanctification of
the Day"), the central benediction in the Sabbath *Amidah.* The
traditional prayer is composed of couplets, in which God is asked
to do something, so that as a consequence, Israel may do something else.

[God,] Satisfy us with your goodness
that we [Israel] may rejoice in your salvation.

[God,] Cleanse our hearts
to serve you in truth.

[God,] In love and grace, give us as our inheritance
your holy Sabbath
that Israel, sanctifiers of your name, may rest on it.

As we see from the last couplet, Shabbat rest is the end, not the means: God gives Israel the Sabbath that Israel may rest. The *Union Prayer Book,* however, turns the logic around: "Help us to preserve the Sabbath as Israel's heritage from generation to generation, that it may ever bring rest and joy, peace and comfort to the dwellings of our brethren, and through it Thy name be hallowed in all the earth." Instead of the Sabbath existing so that Israel, who sanctifies God's name, can rest, the Sabbath provides rest itself (along with peace, joy, and comfort) so that God's name is hallowed. Sanctification has replaced rest as the goal of Shabbat.

Nineteenth-century science thought, wrongly, that it was only a matter of time until scientists would know it all. Larger telescopes and finer microscopes would capture everything for the trained eye to see and to record, while mathematicians would plot the entirety of creation in a brilliantly trenchant set of interlocking equations: the mind of God, as it were, in a few short lines. In such an environment, Reform rabbis were not the only ones intoxicated by the heady taste of truth.

I have often wondered why the generations of Jews my age and younger complain that the *Union Prayer Book* prose is saccharin in its piety. The answer, I think, is that we no longer relate to things in terms of their truths alone. Unable to imagine the spiritual essences of which the nineteenth-century rabbis spoke, we find their rhetoric beautiful but empty.

We are also products of an age that has come to deny the very possibility of achieving the total set of truths that nineteenth-century sciences sought. In 1927, physicist Werner Heisenberg established the observer as part and parcel of that which we observe and, in 1931, mathematician and logician Kurt Goedel demonstrated the impossibility of mathematics ever mapping a coherent and all-encompassing set of truths.

The arts had anticipated this shift. For most of western history, artists struggled to achieve realism. Good art captured the real look of a real thing by ever improving on such objective realities as light, shadow, perspective, and depth. But nineteenth-century impressionists rejected the realists' assumptions that there was such a thing as a single objective reality out there to capture. Reality is transient, they insisted. So in the early 1900's, for instance, Claude Monet painted "the same thing" — ordinary haystacks — over and over again, since it wasn't really the same thing at all, but a different entity from moment to moment as the light and his perspective changed. Cubists like Braque and Picasso took the next step, bravely disassembling human bodies, limb by limb, and saying, in effect, that what we look like is partly how we are looked at. Picasso, it is said, painted a portrait of Gertrude Stein and showed it to Alice B. Toklas. When Toklas objected, "Gertrude doesn't look like that," Picasso retorted, "Don't worry. She will, she will." Similar developments followed in music.

It is as if we have traded in the absolutes of our birthright for a momentary pottage of the temporary and the relative. We hear all the time that morality is relative to individuals or to cultures ("I believe one way; Hitler believed another"). University undergraduates often seem to think that their own view on Hamlet, history, or even the periodic table is as good as their professor's. Steven Goldberg, a professor of Sociology at City University of New York, describes the take-over of the social sciences by "ideologues who act not as if nature is something to be discovered…but, rather, as if she is a handmaiden whose purpose is to satisfy one's psychological and ideological needs." Is nothing for sure any more? Nothing eternal? Are there any absolutes in this mind-world continuum that is continually coming into being?

Morality *is* indeed absolute and unwavering; ritual is not. Even if we cannot agree on what the proper moral stand is, there is such a stand, and our opinion either matches it ("We are right") or it doesn't ("We are wrong").

There *are* also absolute truths. The doctrine of relativity does not imply relativism. On the contrary, it assumes the absolutely unchangeable speed of light. Jumping off the Brooklyn Bridge remains a dangerous thing to do regardless of your opinion on the subject. People who think they can make it all up, as if their mind wholly determines reality, are rightly institutionalized for their own welfare. The issue, then, is not whether we still believe in limits or in truths: All human beings in all ages require both. Our uniqueness as the twentieth century comes to an end lies not in our trashing of limits and of truths, but in our concession that if these are to influence human behavior, they need to be accorded a context of meaning. Religion's task today is the manufacturing of meaning.

The rhetoric of meaning: Shabbat as artistic construct

What is meaning? Meaning is not a quality of any single entity so much as it is an attribute that an entity has by virtue of its connection to another entity. An uncatalogued book by an anonymous author on an unknown subject is meaningless. But give me the author, topic, or call number and I can relate it to other works — file it away as "belonging" somewhere. *Now* it has meaning. A single statistic is meaningless too, but give me the parallel statistic from last year or the equivalent figure for the people next door, and I recognize what the statistic means. Meaning is a relative thing, the importance that a given piece of data has against the backdrop of other data. Things seen in isolation have no meaning at all. What about people in isolation? This question is critical in explaining Shabbat today.

The very essence of modern society is that it progressively releases the individual from the vice-like control of strong limits, and the coercion of the bonded group. But instead of being released to freedom, the individual is drawn into a very difficult social environment. The endemic threat to our existence is precisely the characteristic of living in potential isolation, where we cannot depend on each other, and have little faith in ultimate truth. A life without any social contract at all would be as Thomas Hobbes aptly described it: "nasty, mean, brutish and short." It is total unconnectedness to any social fabric, which is to say, meaninglessness as I have defined it.

To moderns, then, Shabbat is an opportunity for meaning, a moment in time to forge connections and to belong. If Jews will not keep Shabbat on the grounds that they are commanded to do so, or even because Shabbat is an eternal spiritual truth, perhaps they will do so because keeping Shabbat will provide their otherwise disconnected lives with meaning.

Synagogues should elect to become communities of meaning: places people join not for the extrinsic deliverables of the market economy — a rabbi on call, bar/bat mitzvah for a child, or High Holy Day seats annually — but as the way out of anomie. Congregations

53

will have to speak a new language to do that, not the language of fee for services (programs, school schedules, multiple youth groups, and general busyness) but the language of the spirit for those among us who have seen the wilderness. They may be ready to listen anew to the Jewish People's story, including its limits — as the Israelites do in Deuteronomy, hearing the Ten Commandments once again. They will listen because they seek meaning, connectedness to people and to systems, connectedness that goes beyond the facile relationships that even entrepreneurs engage in, connectedness to history, to hope, and to God. Synagogues that herald the message of total engagement with human lives in the making will attract entrepreneurs who are tired of life lived alone on the frontier of meaninglessness. Looking for meaning, they may even find the Sabbath once again.

Precisely because all people in all eras have needed all three things — limits, truth, and meaning — we should not be surprised to find that the Bible itself urges us to ponder meaning, even behind the Ten Commandments themselves. The very first one is, "I am the Lord your God who brought you out of Egypt." What kind of commandment is that, if not the context in which the other nine commandments are intended to find meaning? We do what we do, ultimately, because the God who brought us out of Egypt is real for us.

Our question of Shabbat then boils down to this: Can it become the experience of God's reality? If it can, then keeping it will have the meaning that even the Torah prescribes. If not, as in Salonika centuries back, people will exchange synagogues for Starbucks.

The nature of reality: Shabbat as virtual domain in time

To the best of my knowledge, the late philosopher Susanne K. Langer never studied the Sabbath, but she was a master at the ways in which artistic symbolism functions. Since meaning is an aesthetic impulse to connect things in ways that matter, we might find the answer to our Shabbat question in Langer's view of aesthetics.

Long before computers gave "virtual" a new meaning, Langer used it to describe intangible reality, not just shapes in space, but the shaping *of* space, *of* time, or of any other sensory measure by which we interact with the world. Every mode of art corresponds to its own virtual medium, but the most interesting example is architecture, which Langer calls "virtual domain." A castle creates the domain where royalty is patent. The New York Public Library and the British Museum virtually demand silent respect, even religious veneration, for the collective human mind of the centuries that they house. My home differs from yours in the way that I differ from you. An American teenager's room filled with built-ins, decorated with posters, and littered with books, clothes, food, and other detritus is not the same as a Japanese tea room, with its infinitesimally detailed design. All of these are different architectural wonders, each with its own message of what is real in the universe. We construct them not simply for utilitarian ends but because we want to erect a "spatial semblance of a world."

It is useful to think of Shabbat as virtual domain, a virtual world that Jews build on the master plan of Torah; a world where the presence of God cannot be doubted. But the virtual domain of Shabbat differs from the others since Shabbat is a thing in time, not space. That is the message of Shabbat that Abraham Joshua Heschel leaves us. Shabbat, he says, is "a sanctuary in time." If we superimpose Heschel's analysis of Shabbat in *time* upon Langer's understanding of *virtual domain,* we get Shabbat as a *virtual domain in time, where God's reality is patent.*

The human imagination prefers space to time; it prefers things we can see and touch. We are easily taken in by the idolatry of "thingness," the collectibles that measure what we have accomplished. We like things because we can always add to them. Our spatial possessions are ever increasing. The contents of time, however, are always decreasing. Time reminds us of not of what he have and will some day get, but of what we had and will never have again. "The power we attain in the world of space," says Heschel, "terminates at the border of time [and] time is the heart of existence."

Judaism, however, emphasizes time, not space. In Heschel's words, Judaism is "*a religion of time* aiming at the *sanctification of time.*" Herein lies the essence of Shabbat. It is a completely arbitrary time, the otherwise unremarkable seventh day. "Jewish ritual," he says, "is the architecture of time" and Shabbat is "a palace in time...not a date but an atmosphere."

The Fourth Commandment ⅂

Heschel's "atmosphere" is Langer's "virtual domain." Shabbat requires certain activities (like prayer) and proscribes others (like work) because the regulations establish the atmosphere without which Shabbat does not occur. If no one keeps Shabbat, the atmosphere is never created; the domain never takes shape. Likewise, it is possible to keep Shabbat punctiliously but in such a spiritless way that the atmosphere that such observance is intended to manufacture never arises. Merely abstaining from work without some idea of why such abstinence is necessary may fail to produce the atmosphere of the sacred.

It is necessary to keep Shabbat with the desired atmosphere in mind, the way a pianist must have in mind a larger sound than the note-by-note playing out of the score, or the way a sculptor has a certain shape in mind while executing cuts and gouges on a block of wood.

I said above that meaning is really the same thing as connectedness, the way the number "7" becomes meaningful only when we connect it to the days in the week, the dwarfs in the Snow White story, the number of hills in Rome, or the roll of the dice in a Las Vegas casino. Science, the quintessential search for truth, is also the search for ultimate meaning, perhaps the distillation of the universe into a single all-embracing field theory. Limits also seek out meaning by defining the rules that connect the world's fragmented pieces into a single divine creation. Intuiting God as real is not the same as saying we believe in God. Belief can be difficult, after all, even for things that are empirically demonstrable but are just too vast for minds to capture. Every once in a while, however, things that we have trouble believing attain enough reality to make it hard for us to doubt them.

Take connectedness itself. "I read somewhere," says a character named Ouisa in the play *Six Degrees of Separation,* "that everybody on this planet is separated by only six other people. Six degrees of separation. Between us and everybody else on this planet.... It's not just big names, it's *anyone.* A native in the rain forest, a Tierra del Fuegan, an Eskimo. I am bound to everyone on this planet by a trail of six people. It's a profound thought...how every person is a new door opening up into other worlds."

In the virtual domain of the Sabbath, we become aware of the ultimate connectedness of all that is because the reality of God, who sustains the vastness of it, is incontrovertible. Shabbat is not a solitary endeavor, after all. The commandment is given elsewhere (Exodus 31:16) in the plural: *veshamru venai yisrael et hashabbat,* "the Israelites shall keep the Shabbat" — *all* the Israelites, as a community, together. That is why, for all its accent on private Shabbat rest or meditation, Shabbat also requires public worship, the public reading of Torah, and the public consideration of the prophetic haftarah message. The traditional metaphor portrays Shabbat as a bride, and the time of our Shabbat celebration as the wedding that we all attend together. This sanctuary in time invites us all to see how we are indeed connected by just a few degrees of separation. All of us are guests invited to the family wedding.

Seeing each other, being aware of the finitude of time we share, and certain that a single God inhabits our lives in ways we cannot fathom with our cognitive capacity alone, we become appreciative of the ultimate connectedness of the cosmos and all that it contains. For good reason, Psalm 93, the psalm for Shabbat that was recited in the Temple of old, proclaims, "How great are Your works, O *Adonai,* how very deep are Your designs! A foolish dolt cannot know, a simpleton cannot understand." Shabbat, as sanctuary in time and virtual domain of the sacred, saves us from being foolish dolts and simpletons. On and through Shabbat, we inherit the eyes of William Blake who saw "a World in a Grain of Sand, and a Heaven in a Wild Flower." We live out Martin Buber's I-Thou acknowledgment of all creatures as the meeting place with God.

Ironically, then, far from being the most particularistic commandment, observing Shabbat is simultaneously the most universalistic one. Linked to the cosmic unity inherent in God's creation, it unfolds the potential of an alternative universe of reality, a reality where divisiveness exists no more, where we celebrate time, not space, and where the virtual domain of messianic perfection is ours, at least briefly — a "taste of the world to come," as the liturgy describes it. This is meaningfulness at its best for those of us who yearn for connectedness once again.

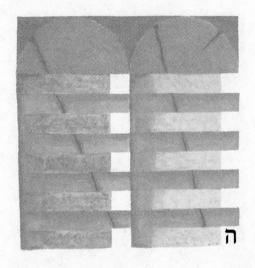

five

כבד את אביך ואת אמך

למען יארכון ימיך

על האדמה

אשר יי אלהיך נתן לך.

Honor your father and mother
that your days may be prolonged
on the soil
that *Adonai* your God is giving you.

The Fifth Commandment

Why does God care how we treat our parents?

There are three partners in the making of a human being: a father, a mother, and the Holy One of Blessing. When we honor our parents, God says, "It is as if I am dwelling among them and they are honoring Me." When we vex our parents, God says, "I am glad not to be living among them; they would no doubt drive Me crazy as well."

The relationship of God and Israel is often expressed in filial terms. "Israel is My first-born son." (Exodus 4:22) "Truly Ephraim is a dear son to Me.... That is why My heart yearns for him; I will receive him back in love." (Jeremiah 31:20) "I fell in love with Israel when he was still a child; and I have called him My son ever since Egypt." (Hosea 11:1) "A son should honor his father, and a slave his master. Now if I am a father, where is the honor due Me?" (Malachi 1:6)

Maimonides teaches: Gratitude for all that our parents have done for us is a stepping stone to recognizing the goodness of God and all the blessings that flow from the Holy One. It is only with a sense of gratitude that our awareness of soul and intelligence become significant.

Holding family and society together

Acknowledgment of parental authority reinforces the fabric of human society as a whole and makes possible the transmission of values and the progress of society. The Hebrew word for honor is *kabed,* which has the same root as the word for "heavy," thus emphasizing the seriousness of this obligation. When Ezekiel upbraids the people for the sins that bring down the nation, failure to honor parents is high on the list: "Every one of the princes of Israel in your midst used his strength for the shedding of blood. Fathers and mothers have been humiliated by you; strangers have been cheated among you; orphans and widows have been wronged in your midst." (Ezekiel 22:6-7)

Honor and fear/revere

In Exodus, the command is to honor (*kabed*) our parents. In Leviticus (19:3), the command is to fear or revere *(tira'u)* them. What is fear and what is honor? Fear means that we do not stand in our parents' place, or contradict them in public, or in any way diminish the esteem due them from others. Honor means that we perform positive acts to help them, bring them joy, and improve their lives, such as provide them with food, drink, and other physical assistance.

The Talmud suspects that we tend to honor our mother more than our father, because our mother sways us with gentle words. When it comes to honor then, the Torah puts "father" first, so we will not diminish the honor due him as well. We traditionally tended to be in awe of our fathers more than our mothers because our fathers were the ones who taught us Torah (or because, in a patriarchal society, they wielded the power). When the Torah commands awe of parents, then, it puts "mother" first so we will not diminish the awe due her as well.

How far should it go?

The Rabbis cite the example of Avimi, whose father asked for a cup of water but fell asleep while his son went to fetch it. Avimi stood by his father's bed and waited with the water until his father woke up. When Rabbi Joseph heard the sound of his mother's footsteps, he would say: "I must rise before the Presence of God *(Shechinah),* which is approaching."

Rabbi Shimon bar Yohai taught: God sets the honor due to parents above even honor due to God. How so? We are commanded to honor God with "substance" (Proverbs 3:9). That is to say, with gleanings, tithes, ritual objects, and taking care of the less fortunate. We are commanded to honor parents in all instances, even if we have no substance to offer, and we have to beg in order to assist them.

Why is there a "reward" for this one?

We are promised that proper parental respect will result in long life in the Land of Promise; when the command is repeated in Deuteronomy, we are told also that things will go well with us for fulfilling this obligation. The modern Bible commentator, Umberto Cassuto, teaches that this reward fits, measure for measure; if you honor the source of your life, you will have life. More compelling, however, is the interpretation found in Gersonides' medieval Torah commentary. He argues that it is not a reward, but rather a natural result. Respect for parents will ensure that succeeding generations will accept the teachings of their elders. The pattern repeats generation after generation, and we live a long life in the values that are perpetuated.

According to the Talmud, there is a reward for honoring parents, and it becomes evident in the World to Come. Our "days will be long" in the world of endless length, and it "will be good" for us in the world that is all good.

What if our parents are not worthy?

In Deuteronomy, the phrase is included, "as *Adonai* your God commanded you." From this, we learn that while we may honor our parents because of deep feeling for them, the mitzvah comes from God, and is binding upon us no matter what our relationship with our parents (although any immoral instructions should be ignored).

Jewish tradition assumes that most parents remain worthy of honor, even though they are flawed. If, however, a parent is mentally ill and it becomes too much for the child to bear, the child may leave the parent in the care of others. While filial obligations do not disappear, it is an acknowledgment that sometimes the behavior of the parents can be seriously detrimental to the welfare of the child, and the child is not condemned to endure it.

Ma'aseh shehayah... It once happened

that there was a young man who fed his father fattened chickens, but when his father asked from where they came, the son replied, "Old man, old man, shut up and eat, even as dogs shut up when they eat." Thus, even though he provided plenty of fine food for his father, he inherited Gehenna (believed to be a place of punishment and purgation for up to twelve months after death, for the purpose of purifying one's soul before entering Paradise). There was another young man whose work was grinding wheat. When the king sent word that millers be brought to work for him, the young man said to his father, "Father, you go in to the mill to grind in my stead, and I will go do the king's work. Should there be humiliation in it, I would rather be humiliated and not you; should there be flogging, let me receive the blows and not you." Thus, though he made his father grind at the mill, the son inherited the Garden of Eden.

What about the obligations of a parent for a child?

The rabbinic literature enumerates some practical obligations of parents for their children — actually, for their sons, but we can apply them to daughters as well. Educate them, provide for them, prepare them to make a living, help them to find a spouse — even teach them to swim! The challenge of parenting, however, is in the way we execute our duties. As Marion Wright Edelman, the head of the Children's Defense Fund, writes to her sons: "I seek your forgiveness for all the times I talked when I should have listened; got angry when I should have been patient; acted when I should have waited; feared when I should have been delighted; scolded when I should have encouraged; criticized when I should have complimented; said no when I should have said yes and said yes when I should have said no. I did not know a whole lot about parenting or how to ask for help. I often tried too hard and wanted and demanded so much, and mistakenly sometimes tried to mold you into my image of what I wanted you to be rather than discovering and nourishing you as you emerged and grew."

— *Rachel S. Mikva*

I Was Young, and I Have Also Grown Older

LEONARD FEIN

A friend tells me the following story regarding his unmarried daughter and the little girl she adopted: One day, several years after the adoption, mother and daughter were romping in bed when the child said, "Mommy, it's not fair." "What's not fair, honey?" "I'm the only one in my whole class who has only a mommy." Pause. "Everybody else has a mommy and a daddy, or two mommies, or two daddies."

Once, the discussion of the commandment focused on the verb: What are the meanings of "honor?" Now, in this unexpected world we inhabit, the nouns, too, have become problematic. Who is your father? Who is your mother? Indeed, my friend's story is no longer particularly noteworthy, not in a season when *The New York Times* reports that one "Kathy Butler, a 47-year-old New Jersey woman, is pregnant with triplets [who] bear no relationship to her or to her husband, Gary, [since] they are growing from ready-made embryos that the Butlers selected and paid for at Columbia-Presbyterian Medical Center in Manhattan."

Jewish tradition is not entirely indifferent to questions of identity. Adoption, after all, created an immediate question, pitting biology against nurture. But, like the question of the "wicked father," issues that were relatively peripheral in earlier times have become critical in our own time. How, indeed, shall we view the commandment in the light of data on the frequency of child abuse? And how, more generally, shall we understand a commandment whose explication in the Talmud includes the following tale:

> The mother of Rabbi Ishmael came to complain
> about her son to the Rabbis, and she said,
> "Rebuke my son, for he does not show me

65

The Fifth Commandment ה

> honor." The faces of the Rabbis grew pale, and
> they said, "Is it possible that Rabbi Ishmael
> should not show honor to his mother? What has
> he done to you?"
>
> She said, "When he goes to the house of study, I
> want to wash his feet and to drink the water
> wherewith I have washed them, and he will not
> permit it."
>
> They said, "Since that is her wish, honor her by
> permitting it."

When I was a child, it seemed quite simple. I took the fifth commandment to be a specific instance of the seventh commandment (against adultery), which I understood as prohibiting offense to adults. Once I outgrew that error, what remained was a somewhat banal admonition. The notion that this was an absolute commandment against "adult"-ery, to which almost no exceptions were allowed, was not available to me. Not merely because the very idea of "commandment" was alien, but because everything I believed about such things was rooted in reciprocity and hence in contingency. Honor your parents, even if they do not "deserve" honor? Honor them in their lapses, in their foibles and their flaws, in their anger and in their sloth? To honor them in this way would be to accept the priority of ascribed status over deserts, and I was raised — by my parents, whom I sometimes honored — to deprecate ascription.

"*Na'ar hayiti vegam zakanti,* I was young, and now I have grown older" — even if, as is so often the case, I have grown older rather too late. Do I not, for example, accept the notion of unconditional love with regard to my children? And what is "unconditional love" if not a love that proceeds from ascription rather than deserts? And if unconditional love for my children, then why not unconditional honor for my parents?

But: Once, during the intermediate days of *Pesach,* my mother, *z"l* (*zichronah livrachah,* may her memory be a blessing) and I went on a trip. At the lunch counter of a drugstore, she ordered a bacon-lettuce-tomato sandwich on toast — and said to me, "Don't tell anyone." I remember little of my mother, who, like the rest of my family, lived very much in my father's shadow. But I remember, powerfully, that sandwich and her admonition. And I remember that something curdled inside me.

Can honor and curdling co-exist? "Honor" speaks to filial behavior, not to filial judgment or sentiment. Maimonides is clear: "It is possible for a man to honor and revere and obey those whom he does not love." Or, by extension, to honor and revere those whom he does not respect. In Freud's wake, we cannot pretend to mindless honor. We are, in fact, encouraged to see our parents as real people, with feet of clay and warts intact. (Have I not encouraged my own daughters so to see me? Did I not once plead with my eldest to understand me as a person and not only as a role — that is, as her father?) But the tradition is not insensitive to the conflict between our feelings and our behavior. It acknowledges the possibility of such conflict, and pointedly tells us that the commandment to honor trumps such intellectual and/or emotional reservations as we may have.

And yes, I sin by telling this story of my mother, by this delayed violation of her instruction. Just as I sinned, wittingly and unwittingly, repeatedly, while my parents were alive. My exculpatory argument (or, at least, my plea for clemency) is that I have, or would like to think I have, honored them in the whole if not in the parts. I am my parents' child. And while I acknowledge that this effort to sweep the details under the rug is a cop-out, I cop right back in with the acknowledgment of the proximity of apple to tree.

• • •

I am struck, as I browse through the sources, by the wisdom of the sages. True, I cannot abide the notion of accepting Rabbi Ishmael's mother's desire to drink the filthy water. (I hope, in fact, that Rabbi Ishmael was sufficiently sensitive so that before he came, barefoot, to bid farewell to his mother on his way to the house of study, he washed his feet quite thoroughly, enabling him to present himself to his mother with clean feet and a pure heart.) But a host of issues that we, in our modernist conceit, regard as peculiarly contemporary are discussed again and again in the sources, from the earliest times. In-laws, and the difference between a husband's relationship with his wife's parents and a wife's with her husband's? It's there, and so is the issue of what is permitted when we've reached the end of our patience because our parents are mentally disturbed. And so, often extensively, nearly every issue we claim for our very own.

Comes the question: Do we learn anything new from studying the old? Does not our modern (or post-modern, if you prefer) wisdom include essentially all that is worthy of the old, and hence render the old redundant? We do not live in a time or place where it is thought appropriate for the children to rise when their parent enters the room, yet that is very explicitly the ancient sensibility. Does that sensibility and all that goes with it recommend itself for reasons other than idle curiosity?

The answer to that question — at least, the answer of one who, following Mordechai Kaplan, the founder of Reconstructionism, does not instinctively give to the past a veto — is, definitively, affirmative. What the past offers us is an ongoing discussion, shaped not only by the discussants' eagerness to bend themselves to the law but, inevitably, by their own time and place. (That is a mildly subversive statement.)

We can also read the sources as if they were utterly timeless, an eighteenth-century rabbi actively encountering a sixth-century colleague. That is surely how many of the latter-day participants perceived the process, and is among the more striking aspects of the literature. Now it is our turn to enter into the discussion.

But, when we do, do we enter it on our own terms? It is one thing to bring to the discussion ideas and perceptions that are richly informed by our own culture and our own psyche. It is quite another to abandon the structure of the discussion, to alter the rules of argument and evidence. Yet our epistemological habits are hard, perhaps impossible, to shake off. And why even try? Surely it is possible to take the sages of old very, very seriously, and to accept that some of them, at least, may have been substantially wiser than we. We can do this without necessarily embracing their methodology. What is wanted and warranted, it seems to me, is a readiness for conversation. Sometimes, the conversation is awkward: Those of us who are not fluent in the language and the culture of the sages may easily feel lost. But even if we are not up to becoming fluent in their language and culture, there are interpreters galore, dead and living, to help us.

Why bother with such a conversation? Is there so much to be learned? Because bothering with such a conversation is quite precisely the principal way we have of fulfilling the commandment, of honoring our mothers and fathers.

I take this as a responsible interpretation of the text. The Levitical version of the fifth commandment: "Each-man — his mother and his father you are to hold-in-awe, and My Sabbaths you are to keep" (Leviticus 19:3) suggests the connection between reverence for one's parents and reverence for the tradition. And in the next chapter, too, we read, "Indeed, any-man, any-man that insults his father or his mother is to be put-to-death..." (Leviticus 20:9) immediately following, "You are to keep My laws, and observe them." The juxtapositions do not absolutely confirm my interpretation, but they are powerfully suggestive — as is the reason we are given for the commandment in its original statement, "...that your days may be prolonged on the soil that Adonai your God is giving you." The plain text implies the literal soil of the Land of Israel, but, in light of our fate in that land, we may not be wide of the mark in reading "soil" as "Torah," the fertile ground of our peoplehood. (And if we are wide of the mark? That is what gives the conversation its bounce.)

So: Honor your father and mother, through whom you are heir to the tradition, by tending to the tradition. And if your literal parents botched the job of inducting you into the tradition? No matter, the commandment is rooted in biology, not pedagogy.

There's the rub. We bridle at biological categories. Not only do they lack scientific foundation; they are laced with the potential for bigotry, they become slogans for justifying murder. And the only way around that that suits the modern temperament — and the Jewish imperative — is to insist that this people is, somehow, an exception. Judaism is not a confessional faith. It is rooted in peoplehood, and, though one can "join" the people through a confessional act, the fundamental category is blood. I write that nervously. I do not like to think it, much less to write it. But I know no way around it.

That said, the fundamental defining characteristic of my relationship with my parents is, again, blood. It is prior to all else, and colors all else. There are amendments, exceptions, adjustments, but

69

the fact remains essentially intractable. We honor our parents because it is they who gave us life. If they are lovable, we may love them. But whether or not they are lovable, we must honor them.

Once, near the end of his days, my father took ill, and it fell to me to stay with him around the clock. I felt imprisoned. I hated him for the imposition, and hated myself for feeling as I did. But I stayed.

Will my children in similar circumstances feel as conflicted toward me as I did toward my father? I have done what I could to alter the family trajectory, but one never knows. On balance, I think we of this generation are better at seeing our children as people, thereby inviting them to see us as people. Perhaps that helps.

• • •

It is time to honor my mother and my father: They were both teachers. My mother mostly taught second grade; by the time I was in third or fourth grade, or perhaps eighth grade, I had little use for second grade teachers. Baby-sitters, I thought. And then once, home from college during vacation, I saw for the first time the collection of professional journals on my mother's night-table. And now and again over the years I've met people who recall that it was she who introduced them to the Hebrew language. My mother, the teacher, who nursed me through my polio, who gave me life.

When my father retired after many years of service as a teacher at the Baltimore Hebrew College, a dinner was tendered in his honor. This is the story he told that night when he was asked to say a few words:

> When I was a boy, the rebbe in our *cheder* (class) in Benderi (Bessarabia) said to us one day, "Children, they say that very far away, there is a country called America, and I suppose that is so, for why would they lie about such a thing? And they say as well that in that far-away country called America, there is a city called Philadelphia, and I suppose that, too, is so. And they go on to say that in the city called Philadelphia, there, is a bell they call the Liberty Bell, and that on that bell are engraved words

from our book: *Proclaim liberty throughout the land and to all the inhabitants thereof.* Frankly, I find that hard to believe. Why would they write our words on their bell?

"I have a favor to ask of you now. If it should happen when you grow up that you go to America, try to visit the place they call Philadelphia and see the bell. And write and tell me whether it is true that they have inscribed our words on their bell. I would like to know such a thing."

As it happened, I did come to America, and I chanced to Philadelphia, and I went to see the bell, and yes, indeed, there were the words, our words. But the bell was cracked.

You honor me tonight for my life as a teacher. I prefer to think of myself as a person who has sought to be a bell-mender.

My father, who taught me about mending the bell, and who gave me life.

six

לא תרצח.

You shall not murder.

The Sixth Commandment

Now we are murderers all

Rabbi Avraham Yitzhak Bloch of Telshe asks: Is murder not a universal crime since it is one of the seven laws given to all people during the time of Noah? Is there any teaching about this commandment that is unique to the children of Israel?

He suggests that a concept of murder more subtle and comprehensive than standard legal definitions is intended. In the Talmud we learn that if we publicly embarrass someone, it is considered as if we shed blood because shame causes people's blood to drain from their face.

Certainly a bit of gossip or criticism cannot be considered murder in any real sense. But then we have to admit that for most of us, the most profound pain ever caused us by other human beings was done with words...and in some cases, we still bear the wounds.

Other kinds of assaults against people are also seen as murderous. Some, like rape, obviously destroy aspects of life that cannot be recovered. Some require a greater stretch of our imagination. If you cause people to lose their livelihood, the Talmud says it is as if you murder them. If you pretend to be a scholar and hand down halachic decisions without having attained the proper level of wisdom, or if you have the knowledge and experience yet refrain from teaching — you strike down many students. Even a host who fails to provide travelers with sufficient provisions and an escort to ensure their safety is described as a shedder of blood.

While the punishment for these transgressions is not like the punishment for murder — in fact many have no punishment at all — the teachings make abundantly clear our obligation to protect and enrich the lives of others in all circumstances.

What about the death penalty?

The debate about capital punishment is an ancient one. While the Torah identifies several capital crimes (including first-degree murder), the Rabbis created such strict rules of evidence that it became nearly impossible to sentence a criminal to death. In the Talmud, it is written: A Sanhedrin (the supreme rabbinic court) that orders an execution once in seven years is branded a destructive tribunal. Rabbi Eliezer ben Azariah says: Once in seventy years. Rabbi Tarfon and Rabbi Akiva say: Were we members of a Sanhedrin, no person would *ever* be put to death. Such an absolute stand disturbed Rabban Simeon ben Gamaliel. With no threat of the death penalty, he feared, shedders of blood in Israel would multiply.

What about suicide or euthanasia?

The taking of all life, even our own, is seen as a crime against God. In the verse, "For your own life-blood I will require a reckoning" (Genesis 9:5), the Rabbis hear a prohibition of suicide. The sanctity of all human life, whether old or young, weak or vital, resonates in God's creation of us "in the Divine image."

While Jewish tradition forbids any action that hastens death, we are not compelled to hopelessly prolong it either. Active euthanasia is forbidden, but there is great compassion for those who are suffering. The Talmud tells this story to illustrate the delicate balance:

> When Rabbi Judah haNasi (also known simply as "Rabbi" in Talmudic literature) became deathly ill, all of the rabbis began to pray without cease for his recovery. His handmaid ascended the roof and prayed: "The immortals [angels] desire Rabbi to join them, and the mortals desire Rabbi to remain with them; may it be the will of God that the mortals overpower the immortals." When, however, she saw how much pain and distress he was in, she prayed: "May it be the will of the Almighty that the immortals overpower the mortals."
>
> Yet the rabbis' incessant prayers seemed to hold him here on earth, so she took up a jar and threw it down from the roof to the ground. For a split second, it interrupted their prayers, and the soul of Rabbi departed to its eternal rest.

Pikuah nefesh... The saving of life

Rabbi Yehuda teaches in the name of Samuel: "Keep My decrees and laws, since it is only by keeping them that a person can truly live" (Leviticus 18:5). The intent is clearly that you should live by the commandments, not die on account of them.

It is commanded that we violate any precept of the Torah in order to save life, except three: murder, idolatry, or adultery. Self-defense is allowed, even mandatory, but we may not murder someone who does not directly threaten us, as in the case that came before Raba: A man testified, "The governor of my town has ordered me, 'Go and kill so-and-so. If you do not, I will kill you.'" Raba answered, "Let him kill you so that you do not commit murder; what cause do you have to believe that your blood is redder [that is, that your life is more worthy]?"

The bloods of your brother...

When Cain murders Abel, God declares that the bloods of his brother cry out from the ground. In the plural, it teaches that each murder kills not only the victim, but all the future children and all the creative work yet to be done by that individual as well.

Destroying (or saving) the entire world

The Torah describes the creation of a single soul at the beginning of the human race to teach us that if we murder one human being, it is as if we destroy the entire world. On the other hand, if we are able to save one person, it is as if we preserve the entire world. A single ancestor was created for the sake of peace, so that no one can say to another: My lineage is greater than yours! It also proclaims the greatness of the Holy One of Blessing. For if a man strikes many coins from a single mold, they all resemble each other. But God fashions all of us from the mold of the first human, yet not one of us is just like another. Therefore each of us is obliged to say: The whole world was created for my sake.

Murder becomes impossible

The modern philosopher, Emmanuel Levinas, teaches that if we look at the Other and recognize the existence of a being outside ourselves ("see his face"), killing becomes impossible. "You shall not murder" does not conform with our normal relationship to things, in which we see them like "nourishment," how they can fill our need for self-contentment, self-enjoyment, or self-knowledge. Seeing the face of the other submerges murderous intent and inaugurates our spiritual journey.

Even if we are not guilty, we may be responsible

According to the Talmud, if it is in our power to protest against the wickedness of others, but we do not protest, we are not regarded as thoroughly righteous. Abraham Joshua Heschel echoes this warning:

> There is an evil which most of us condone and are even guilty of: indifference to evil. We remain neutral, impartial, and not easily moved by the wrongs done to other people. Indifference to evil is more insidious than evil itself.... A silent justification, it makes possible an evil erupting as an exception becoming the rule.... The decay of conscience fills the air with a pungent smell. Good and evil, which were once as distinguishable as day and night, have become a blurred mist. But that mist is man-made. God is not silent. He has been silenced.

— *Rachel S. Mikva*

Undoing Creation

LEVI WEIMAN-KELMAN

> The Torah was revealed not only to the Jews.
> God revealed the Torah to all the nations of the
> world. God first approached the children of Esau.
> "Will you accept the Torah?" God offered. "What
> does the Torah contain?" they asked. "You shall
> not murder." "Master of Infinity," they said, "the
> very essence of our ancestor (Esau) is murder-
> ous. His own father promised that he would live
> by his sword" *(Genesis 27:40)*.
>
> There was not a single nation to whom God did
> not go and, as it were, knock on its door, asking
> whether it would be willing to accept the Torah.
> As with the children of Esau, some fundamental
> aspect of their characters or heritage made them
> refuse. At long last, God came to Israel. They said,
> "We will do and we will hearken" *(Exodus 24:7)*.

Growing up, I had a sense that the sixth commandment wasn't
even meant for Jews because Jews were existentially incapable of
murder. Jewish moral sensitivity would not allow us to stand by
while innocents were slaughtered. It was unthinkable that Jews
could participate in or perpetrate such crimes. Our lack of political sovereignty allowed us the luxury of regarding the abuses of
power by our host nations with contempt. Many Jews felt that the
murderous nature of the non-Jewish world was fully revealed as we
became the primary victims of the greatest violation of the sixth
commandment in human history. We, who had brought the world
"You shall not murder," fell victim to the murderers.

The commandment became reinterpreted as "You shall not be murdered." We shall not allow others to murder us. In a sense Zionism, especially after the Shoah (the Holocaust), was the fulfillment of this command, a response to having allowed ourselves to be murdered. Many believed that experiencing the Shoah would protect us from becoming like our oppressors, even as we achieved sovereignty and power. We believed our suffering would serve as a kind of moral vaccine, preventing us from causing suffering.

Yet we have not mastered either formulation. Fifty years after the Shoah, Baruch Goldstein (may his name be erased), murdered unarmed Moslems in prayer at the Cave of the Patriarchs in Hebron in 1994. Not long after that, another Jew (Yigal Amir) murdered Israeli Prime Minister Yitzhak Rabin *(z"l)*. Perhaps it seems blasphemous to mention the systematic extermination of six million Jews in the same sentence with the murder of twenty-nine Palestinians and one Jew. Murder and genocide are not equal crimes. However, the small but significant cult that venerates both Goldstein and Amir reminds us that no people has evolved completely beyond the capacity for killing.

The Torah itself literally screams out the message that the murderous impulse is part of existential human experience. A quick survey of Biblical siblings reveals Cain murdering Abel, Esau wanting to murder Jacob, and Joseph the victim of attempted murder by his brothers. Shimon and Levi murder all the men of Shechem to avenge the rape of their sister. King David sends Uriah to his death so that he may take this faithful soldier's wife.

Women are not immune to the murderous impulse. Isaac is too young to feel threatened by his older brother Ishmael, so it falls to Sarah to do his attempted murder for him; she banishes Hagar and Ishmael to the desert. Yael murders the enemy captain, Sisera, by driving a tent peg through his skull. And there is always Jezebel, one of the most bloodthirsty characters in the Bible, seeking to promote her ideas and accomplish her goals by killing all those who stand in her way. The list goes on.

God knows this violence is in each of us. Before the first murder is even committed, God warns Cain: "If you do right, there is uplift. But if you do not do right, sin crouches at the door" (Genesis 4:7). This, the first moral instruction, charges us to make choices based on right and wrong, not simply on God's commandment. And we fail. Heartbroken at God's rejection of his sacrifice and seething at the obvious favor in God's eyes that Abel has received, "Cain said to his brother Abel...and when they were in the field, Cain set upon his brother Abel and killed him" (Genesis. 4:8).

We were about to hear the first conversation between the first siblings, but the words are not there. What did Cain say to Abel? The silence of the text is deafening. Perhaps it was something Abel said that led to the murder. Did he gloat? Perhaps it was something that wasn't said. Sforno teaches that we express our feelings through words. When words fail, as perhaps they did here, we resort to violence. Cain could not express his anger in words; he could only act on it.

God laments, "What have you done? *Kol demei achicha tso'akim eilai min ha'adamah.* The cry of your brother's blood screams to Me from the earth!" (Genesis. 4:10). There is a striking contrast between the silence of the brothers before the murder, and Abel's blood crying out after. Cain has nothing to say, yet the earth "opens its mouth" to receive Abel's blood and to bewail the enormity of the loss. Alienated from this earth, Cain can no longer till the soil and he is condemned to a nomadic existence.

The power of words spoken and not spoken is revealed in the very fabric of the universe. In the first chapter of Genesis, the cosmos emerges from speech. The Torah opens with words spoken by God — each divine utterance an act of creation. Speech creates order out of chaos: God said...and there was. Words create worlds. "God said: Let the earth bring forth..." (Genesis. 1:24) and life emerges.

No wonder the earth itself is traumatized by the murder of Abel. The blood pouring into the ground is a reversal of the act of the creation of Adam. Each murder releases a cry from nature, a cry that reaches the divine. It expresses the panic that creation is being undone and the cosmos is reverting to chaos. Human silence in the face of murder resounds over against the creative power of divine speech.

As human history unfolds, we learn more and more how we enhance or destroy God's creation with words, performing limitless acts of virtue with our power of speech, and unconscionable feats of destruction. The Hebrew word for speech or tongue, *lashon* לשון, is very instructive. Its first letter *(lamed)* points upward, indicating that language can be used to elevate humanity and draw us closer to God: blessing, prayer, Torah. The final *nun* at the end, however, points downward and drops low, indicating that speech can also drag us down and degrade life. Judah Loew of Prague taught: Speech is like the fruit of a tree. One can know the nature of the tree from the fruit it produces...."

Can words save the brothers now — Arabs and Jews — both descendants of Abraham? Silence can teach us only about the blood spilled and the sacrifices made, as in the poem, "And My Brother Said Nothing." Written by the Israeli poet, Amir Gilboa, it has become a common text for *Yom Hazikaron* ceremonies (Memorial Day for fallen Israeli soldiers):

> My brother came back from the field dressed in gray. And I was afraid that my dream might prove false, so at once I began to count his wounds. And my brother said nothing.
>
> Then I rummaged in the pockets of the trench-coat and found a field dressing, stained and dry. And on a frayed postcard, her name — beneath a picture of poppies. And my brother said nothing.
>
> Then I undid the pack and took out his belong-ings, memory by memory. Hurrah, my brother, my brother the hero, now I've found your decora-tions! Hurrah, my brother, my brother the hero, I shall proudly hymn your name! And my brother said nothing. And my brother said nothing.
>
> And his blood was crying out from the ground.

It is a modern Israeli midrash, reinterpreting the biblical tale of Cain and Abel as it expresses the relationship between the fallen and those who survive. We have paid a price for our return to the land. It is soaked with the blood of the fallen. We, too, live by the sword, just as surely as the descendants of Esau. The earth cries out, and human silence is death. But not all words can save.

"Life *and* death are in the power of the tongue" (Proverbs 18:21). The implicit connection between words and murder becomes increasingly explicit. In a rabbinic interpretation, the tongue is compared to an arrow: "Why not to another weapon, a sword for example? Because if a man unsheathes his sword to kill his friend, and his friend pleads with him and begs for mercy, the man may be mollified and return the sword to its scabbard. But an arrow, once it is shot, cannot be returned, no matter how much one wants to." Hurtful words, once spoken aloud, cannot be withdrawn before doing real harm. Destructive words, once spoken in public, are no longer under our control.

Nor can we control how words of hate lead to acts of hate. In turning the creative power of speech on its head, we release forces of destruction. The continued demonization of Arabs (a staple of Israeli propaganda for so many years) certainly led to Baruch Goldstein's murderous assault, just as surely as the demonization of Israel in the Arab press has provoked continued violence. For some right-wing religious authorities to name Prime Minister Rabin (z"l) a *rodef,* a "pursuer," made it halachically "acceptable" to murder him. (In Jewish law, it is permissible to kill in self-defense. If someone is "pursuing" you and threatening your life, you must take action. The rabbis who argued that Rabin was a *rodef* said that his policies put the lives of Israeli citizens in jeopardy.) The malicious use of speech against "the other" has, at one time or another, legitimized the oppression of Jews, gypsies, African-Americans, homosexuals, communists, Protestants, Catholics, Muslims — and the list goes on. Silence in the face of such sinful speech is death.

But there have been spoken words of peace as well. Acknowledgment and accords. Promises and progress. Like Cain, we receive fair warning: If you do right, there is uplift. But if you do not do right, sin crouches at the door. So we go out into the field and say to our brother....

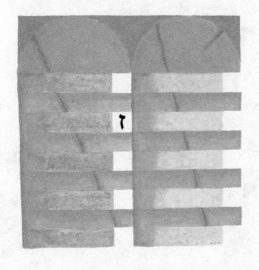

seven

לא תנאף.

You shall not commit adultery.

The Seventh Commandment

Ma'aseh shehayah... It once happened

that a woman went every Shabbat to listen to Rabbi Meir's discourse. Her husband never went along; he did not think much of such teachings. One week, Rabbi Meir went on at great length and when the woman got home late, her husband was furious. He yelled at his wife: "Don't come back home unless and until you have spat in that man's eye!" The woman stayed away from home for three weeks. Finally, friends convinced her to go to Rabbi Meir's lecture again. Perhaps he could help. With divine inspiration, Rabbi Meir immediately understood the situation. In the middle of his lecture, he asked: "Is there someone who can whisper a charm over my eye? It pains me."

The woman's friends convinced her to go forward. They told her to whisper in his ear and spit lightly in his eye, so she could live with her husband again. When she came close to Rabbi Meir, she confessed that she had no idea how to whisper such a charm. "Nevertheless," he insisted, "spit in my face seven times, and I will be healed." She did it, and he told her, "Now go tell your husband that you spat in my face seven times!"

Rabbi Meir's students were disturbed. How could such a great teacher submit to such disgrace? When he explained the situation, they were not satisfied. Still, it would have been better to bring the husband forward for punishment for such cruelty! "No," said Rabbi Meir. "If God allows the Divine Name to be blotted out for the sake of peace between husband and wife [by writing the Name and dissolving it in the 'bitter waters,' an ordeal to prove the innocence of a wife suspected of adultery], I can surely suffer a little indignity for the same purpose."

We lose what we have

Our masters teach: Those who are unfaithful set their eyes upon something that is not theirs. In their infidelity, they do not get what they seek; instead what they had possessed is taken away from them.

Fidelity is more than skin deep

Resh Lakish warns: Don't suppose that only the ones who commit the act with their bodies are called adulterers. Those who commit it merely with their eyes are also called adulterers. Similarly, any violation of the sanctity of the relationship, whether it be by dishonesty, abuse, or disinterest can be considered adultery.

Our relationship with our spouse reflects our relationship with God

"You must not commit adultery" is parallel to the commandment not to commit idolatry; each is in the second position on its tablet. Someone who betrays the marital relationship can be expected to betray God. The prophets certainly understand the power of this analogy, as they invoke images of Israel as an unfaithful wife. God reveals to Hosea:

> For she is not My wife and I am not her husband.
> Let her put away her harlotry from her face,
> and her adultery from between her breasts....
>
> I will punish her for the days of the Baalim on
> which she brought them offerings;
> When bedecked with earrings and jewels, she
> would go after her lovers
> Forgetting Me, declares the Lord. *(Hosea 2:4, 15)*

The pathos of the covenantal relationship violated is profound. Hosea, after he marries a prostitute, comes to experience the pain of God's heartbreak. Yet there is an equally moving vision of fidelity: "I will espouse you forever. I will espouse you with righteousness and justice, with goodness and mercy. I will espouse you with faithfulness." (Hosea 2:21-22).

Suborning adultery

Even if we assist in arranging the rendezvous, we can be considered guilty of adultery. While the teaching is not intended literally, we recognize that there is much complicity in marital affairs today: people who know it is going on and say nothing, people who figure it is nobody's business. The "public" has no right to know, but friends who do know have a right and a responsibility to remind their wayward acquaintances of the vow they took.

Weakening of love

A proverb: When our love was strong, we could lie on the edge of a sword together. Now that it has grown weak, a bed ninety feet wide is not big enough for us. Rabbi Huna said: It is the same with God and Israel. In the beginning, God said, "I will meet with you there and speak with you from above the Ark cover" (Exodus 25:22), and that is a space of less than three feet. In the time of Solomon, however, our meeting place became less intimate; the Temple was over three thousand square feet, and forty-five feet high. Now there is no place big enough: "The heaven is My throne and the earth My footstool. Where is the house that you can build for Me?" (Isaiah 66:1).

From the *ketubah*

Be consecrated unto me as my wife (or husband) in accordance with the traditions of Moses and Israel. I will honor and cherish, support and sustain you, as Jewish husbands (or wives) have honored and cherished, supported and sustained their wives (or husbands) with faithfulness.

A consuming fire

When the presence of God dwells between husband and wife, they are blessed. When God is not present, the fires of passion destroy them. The Divine Name יה (YaH) draws together the י in איש (*iysh*, man) with the ה in אשה (*ishah*, woman), but if they drive out the saving power of God's love from their midst, the י and the ה depart, leaving only אש (*eish*), a consuming fire.

On a billboard in Dallas

Loved the wedding. Invite Me to the marriage.

— God

— *Rachel S. Mikva*

Sacred Boundaries

PETER S. KNOBEL

Positioned between *You shall not murder* and *You shall not steal* is the seventh commandment: *Lo tin'af* — *You shall not commit adultery.* The Torah seems to be saying that if we improperly cross the boundary of intimacy, it destroys something more significant than property rights, something almost as sacred as human life itself — but not quite.

In the wedding ceremony bride and groom declare, "Be sanctified to me as my husband (or as my wife)...in accordance with the tradition of Moses and Israel." The basic meaning of the Hebrew root *kds*, "sanctified," is to be set apart. From that moment forward, the couple asserts, they will share the most intimate aspect of themselves only with each other as the ultimate expression of love and fidelity. "I am my beloved's and my beloved is mine" (Song of Songs 6:3). Recognizing that sexual intimacy is fraught with danger and pregnant with possibility, Jewish tradition draws boundaries. We are commanded to control our sexual appetites, channel our desires into appropriate relations, and preserve the family as the locus of safe human intimacy. We are invited to see that love sanctified by the rituals of *chupah* (marriage canopy) and *kiddushin* (literally "holinesses," the ceremony of betrothal) brings the presence of God into the bedroom; and in the act of making love, husband and wife can become "one flesh."

Judaism envisages marriage as the ideal relationship. "It is not good for man to be alone," God declares in Genesis (2:18), and the *midrash* portrays the Holy One as officiating at Adam and Eve's wedding in the Garden of Eden. The very first pairing of humanity moves beyond biological function into a sacred relationship.

Even more significant theologically is that the relationship between God and the Jewish people is depicted as a marriage. God acts as the husband and Israel as the wife, with the Torah as their *ketubah* (marriage contract) and Mount Sinai stretched over their heads like a wedding canopy. Heaven and Earth stand as witnesses to the sacred covenant, and God brooks no rivals.

By drawing a parallel between the relationship of husband and wife to that of God and Israel, adultery and idolatry become kindred sins. They both violate a unique covenantal bond whose exclusivity defines its *kedushah* (holiness), and whose commitment demands a lifetime of faithfulness. It is the involvement of God in the relationship that raises marriage to a level of unique sanctity, and adultery to a uniquely severe desecration.

So severe a violation of our values and our faith, adultery is assigned the death penalty. It is unlikely that this rule was enforced, but as Rabbi Daniel Schiff teaches, it may not matter:

> Time and again the Torah, in both its written and oral forms, threatens dire punishments that are never intended to be carried out. The aim, rather, is to convey an unambiguous message about the values of Jewish society and the critical interest of the body politic in embracing certain behaviors and rejecting others. Overblown punishments are threatened in order to communicate just how menacing a particular infraction is seen to be to the welfare of Jewish civilization. Once the punishment has been stated, enforcement methods become largely academic; breaking the law and inviting the predetermined wrath of society — even if empirically that wrath almost never comes — is sufficiently distasteful to most people to make the educational arm of the law powerful indeed.

The power of the threat, however, depends on obedience as the rule, and general acceptance of the underlying value. One of the threatened consequences of adultery was the *sotah* ordeal, in which a wife suspected of adultery was tested by the drinking of bitter waters. If she was guilty, her belly would swell up and her thigh fall away. By the time of the *Mishnah,* this ritual was officially discontinued — not because it was seen as too harsh or sexist or magical, but ostensibly because the men themselves were too promiscuous and thereby made the test ineffectual. As violations of sacred intimacy increased, the moral power of the law also diminished.

Today, liberal Jews have largely eliminated the concept of sin from their vocabulary and especially from their moral reasoning. We tend to "understand," or psychologize adultery. We investigate the roots of the deteriorated relationship and provide emotional support for the parties involved, but rarely condemn the sinful behavior. As rabbis have increasingly become pastors more than teachers and adjudicators, even the pulpit responds to adultery with a deafening silence. Most Reform rabbis will marry couples whose projected unions are the result of adulterous affairs. (The Israeli and British Reform movements, however, state that rabbis should not officiate under these circumstances and there are some rabbis in this country urging a similar position.) In no instance do we deprive the adulterer or adulteress of an honored place within the community.

Have the sacred boundaries shifted?

Eugene Borowitz, in his book, *Choosing a Sex Ethic: A Jewish Inquiry,* recognizes that the sexual revolution made sexual boundaries seem elusive. Especially in liberal Judaism, which recognizes personal autonomy as characteristic of the modern personality, decision-making became more complex. Borowitz offers four ethical positions regarding sexual relationships, and provides the tools for considering our behavior: 1) healthy orgasm, 2) mutual consent, 3) love, 4) marriage. While clearly supporting marriage as the Jewish ideal, he acknowledges that many individuals adopt the other ethical positions consciously or unconsciously.

Central to Borowitz's argument is that ultimately, for a Jew, ethics are a necessary but not sufficient condition for choosing a particular behavior. The serious Jew's autonomy is limited by what Borowitz calls the "Jewish autonomous self." Judaism makes a special claim on us. Autonomy does not function in a vacuum. Recognizing an ideal creates a hierarchy of ethical positions.

In Judaism, lifelong procreative monogamous marriage is not simply an option among intimate relationships, not only an ideal. It is a *mitzvah* — a sacred obligation. Its purpose is two-fold: procreation and personal fulfillment. Marriage creates family, which is the locus for the preservation of Judaism and the Jewish people. In this setting, sexual intercourse is a religious act equivalent to prayer or Torah study, and the home becomes a holy place. It is a societal, communal, and personal expectation. The liberal Jewish community faces a complex dilemma because it wishes to be inclusive and pastoral. Therefore, stressing the obligatory nature of marriage in Judaism is often interpreted as hurtful to those who are not married, making them feel excluded. Clearly there is a need for a caring and sensitive response on the part of clergy and synagogues, but this response does not require relinquishing the ideal. While singles, divorce(e)s, widow(er)s, and childless couples need more support from the synagogue, so do families. Many forces threaten to pull them apart.

Until recently, the Jewish divorce rate was low; now it approaches the almost fifty percent average of the rest of the United States. Our synagogues are populated by single heads of households, and our religious schools by children who spend alternate weekends with their divorced parents. Recent studies document the devastating effect of divorce on children and the frequent impoverishment of women. The dissolution of the family in inner cities is cited as a major factor in the decline of entire communities. While Jewish tradition recognizes that divorce is sometimes necessary, it poignantly suggests that God weeps every time a marriage breaks down.

Long-term marriage requires a tremendous amount of nurturing. Fidelity is a spiritual commitment as well as a physical one. Often our occupations or our leisure activities become all-consuming passions that distance us from our spouses and our children, with as devastating an effect on the family as physical adultery. The proliferation of literature and therapeutic programs to revive lost intimacy indicates our growing concern with "spiritual infidelity."

Lifelong commitment to a spouse is now complicated by increased longevity, and by the emphasis in our society on personal fulfillment. Marriage requires more emotional commitment than many are willing to make. Relationships become obsolete in an age of rapidly changing technology and the need for constant and immediate gratification. A marriage in such a society easily becomes as dispensable as last year's computer.

This is the marital terrain on which Judaism makes its stand: Adultery is (still) a sin, and as a religious community, we condemn it.

The privatization of morality tempts us to dismiss sexual behavior as a personal matter. We abhor the notion of society looking into our bedrooms. However, few in our society would sanction incest (which, in Jewish tradition, is a form of adultery). It remains a crime. Our abhorrence of incest is visceral; we know that it is wrong. We do not equivocate and we show little sympathy or empathy for people who engage in incest, especially when the victims are children. Even in the case of consenting adults, we believe that it transgresses a boundary that should not be crossed. So the right to privacy is not absolutely sacrosanct, and when we see the havoc that the breakdown of the family causes, we know private behavior has public consequences.

Judaism reminds us that the line between private and public is sometimes very thin. Even our choice of sexual partners is a matter of communal concern. The seventh commandment is about family and its preservation. Family is the basic unit of society. It provides, food, shelter, education, and identity. It tells to whom we are related by biology and marriage. We are so-and-so's child or sibling or parent or spouse. Ideally, we love the members of our family and the home is where we are safe. But family is also a social and an economic unit, responsible for supporting its members, raising its children, and contributing to the welfare of the community. Identities, rights of inheritance, emotional and economic security are all bound in the bond of matrimony, and violating this sanctified promise results not only in emotional chaos, but also in legal, financial, and communal instability. What happens in families has a profound effect upon society as a whole.

The boundaries cannot shift.

In Jewish thought, the stakes are even higher. We cannot forget that our behavior is judged by two standards: one societal, which is strictly human; and the second revealed, which somehow involves the Divine. This is a central Jewish religious principle. As Jews we believe that morality is more than convention. Our relationships with others affect our relationship with the Divine. Rabbi Arnold

Jacob Wolf reminds us that "the divorce of human obligation from responsibility to God is dangerous and un-Jewish."

How we conduct our intimate relationships is of profound Jewish concern. Judaism is lived out in the kitchen, in the work place, and in the bedroom. By the way we conduct our lives, we can raise the ordinary to the level of the holy.

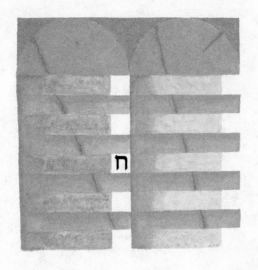

ח

eight

לא תגנב.

You shall not steal.

The Eighth Commandment

Ma'aseh shehayah... It once happened

that a man and his daughter received $400 additional cash from an ATM machine. The father planned to return the money to the bank in the morning, but he was curious what his daughter would do if it was up to her. "I would return it," she replied, "unless I really needed it." The second part of the sentence broke his heart.

This lesson stuck with the daughter, and when she grew to become a rabbi, she would often ask teenagers and their parents what they would do in such a situation. The answers say much about our power of rationalization. (As suggested in the movie, *The Big Chill,* rationalizations may be more important to us than sex: "Have you ever gone a week without a rationalization?")

Some replied, "It's the bank's responsibility to keep the machines in working order. If they fail, it's their own fault." Others tried, "It's so little money for a bank; no one is hurt by keeping it." Or "You know they charge for every little transaction, even to get our own money back from them. This is payback." One student tried to justify it in a way he hoped the rabbi would accept: "I would keep it, but give some of it to *tzedakah* [charity]."

Some said they would return the money. The most striking answer of all came from a mother, who suddenly saw herself as teacher of ethics to her children and realized in the most concrete way a parent can that what we do matters. She replied, "I would now."

Steal what?

Rabbinic sources contend that this pronouncement must refer to kidnapping (the stealing of persons), to be on the same level as the other capital offenses mentioned in the decalogue. After all, monetary theft is prohibited in Leviticus 19:11. But interpreters of this "word" also recognize that its tremendous gravity can be discovered in the vast reaches of its command, by extending to

99

all kinds of material, intellectual, and spiritual theft. There are restrictions against excessive profit and lending on interest. We are required to respond to a greeting in appropriate fashion and respect the intellectual property of others, giving credit for borrowed ideas. We cannot steal people's feelings or opinions by cheating and deception *(genevat da'at)*, causing them to have excessively high opinion of us, or to feel grateful when we are undeserving. We cannot take from others their self-esteem.

Partners to the crime

If we borrow without permission or do not make an effort to restore lost property, it is as if we become thieves. We are also prohibited from buying stolen goods, because it encourages thieves to steal and we become partners to the crime.

How far does it go?

When the people of Nineveh seek to repent, the king commands: "Let them turn everyone from his evil way and from the violence that is in their hands." (Jonah 3:8) What is the meaning of "from the violence that is in their hands?" Shmuel says: Even if someone took a single beam of wood that did not belong to him and built it into a palace, he must demolish the entire palace — all of it — and return the beam to its owner. Anything "in our hands" that is not rightfully ours must be returned.

This extreme is balanced by other Talmudic discussions that take into consideration damage to the house and the likely changes to the beam. Still, it does not matter how small an amount is stolen, even if it is the value of a penny. If we take what it not ours from any person, we violate the prohibition.

A thief and a robber

The disciples of Rabbi Johanan ben Zakkai ask him why the Torah is more severe on a stealthy thief than on a brazen daylight robber. It runs counter to our instincts (and to American law, in which robbery is the more serious crime because of the potential for bodily harm in a direct assault). Yet there is a compelling logic in the Talmudic code: A robber who steals directly from a person is equally defiant of God (who sees all) and human beings (who can see only what is in front of them). A thief in the night, on the other hand, seems more afraid of being caught by humans than by God, adding a sort of heresy to his sins. Quoting Isaiah (29:15), ben Zakkai exclaimed, "Ha! Those who would hide their plans deep from the Lord! Who do their work in dark places and say, 'Who sees us and who takes note of us?'"

— *Rachel S. Mikva*

A Bit of a Thief

RICHARD N. LEVY

"Thou Shalt Not Steal!" What a majestic ring these words have. What a paean to the inviolability of private property!

For most of us, stealing is an easy crime to inveigh against. We usually see ourselves as the victims of theft, not its perpetrators, and we sternly lecture our children if we catch them shoplifting. Yet we sometimes fail to correct a bank error in our favor "because the bank makes too much anyway." We may pay half-price for our child's ticket "because he's barely thirteen." We may neglect to declare all sources of income on our taxes "because the government gets enough of our hard-earned money." Are these not examples of stealing, despite our rationalizations?

The prohibition against stealing extends even to non-material thefts, which we hardly think of as stealing at all — to keep other people waiting, thus stealing their time; to forget to credit the author of an idea or a felicitous expression, thus stealing their creativity. In its most serious form, this is plagiarism. But even in its minor form, it violates the Talmudic injunction to speak an idea *beshem omro,* "in the name of its speaker." When we mislead someone or flatter a person dishonestly, we are guilty of *genevat da'at,* stealing a bit of their knowledge; and when we gossip, engaging in *lashon hara,* the language of hurt, we are stealing from someone's reputation.

Rationalization sets in again. Keep people waiting? When I do that, it's usually because I try to cram too many appointments into too short a time. But why don't I schedule fewer people? Well, I rationalize, I let people down if I can't meet with them (forgetting that I let them down more if I'm late, suggesting that they're not important enough for me to be on time for them). Most of us condemn plagiarism, but we may think nothing of it when we fail to give someone credit for a phrase or a little idea. Chances are that whomever we were talking with didn't know the original "author" anyway. If we mislead someone or flatter them, most of the time we're just trying to keep from hurting them. And gossip? Everybody gossips! People talk behind our backs, so why shouldn't we talk behind theirs? Besides, since most of us are down on ourselves, we expect putting other people down will make us feel better. (Of course, when we encounter the individuals we've been belittling, it's hard to relate to them as we did before, and so we dissemble. That adds to the sin of *lashon hara,* the sin of *genevat da'at.* The result: *averah goreret averah,* "one sin attracts another.")

Our self-justifications are of no avail. Does God not say, without qualification: *Lo tignov,* "Thou shalt not steal?" Look at the company this commandment keeps: right up with *lo tirtzach* (Thou shalt not murder), and with *lo tin'af* (Thou shalt not commit adultery) — two of the three crimes (public idolatry is the third) that one may not violate even if threatened with death. All through the rabbinic sources, the gravity of this sin is amplified:

- Let the property of every human being be as precious to you as your own.
- Said Rabbi Yochanan: When people rob even as little as a *perutah* (the smallest denomination), it is as though they had taken the owner's life.
- God did not decree punishment for the generation of the Flood until they began to steal.
- Shmuel said: Even if someone took a single beam of wood that did not belong to him and built it into a palace, he must demolish the entire palace — all of it — and return the beam to its owner.
- If someone has consumed stolen food, the thief can never return it — even the wholly righteous are unable to return it.

Suppose a *perutah* was the only money a person had. To steal it would be equivalent to taking a person's sole livelihood, or to taking that person's life. No wonder stealing is up there with murder! Indeed, stealing is worse. To steal, one passage above argues, is to condemn the whole world to destruction, just as in the Flood. So bad is stealing that it is a crime for which *teshuvah* (repentance) is very difficult in this life, and in the case of stolen food, impossible.

But the Talmud does not always seem to take theft so seriously:

> Thieves once broke in and stole some rams
> owned by the renowned Talmudic sage Rava.
> When the thieves tried to return them, he
> rebuffed their attempt. The great sage Rav had
> ruled that if thieves break in, steal something,
> and escape, they are exempt from punishment
> because they acquired the property with their
> blood, since the owner might have killed them.

Rava and Rav appear to admire the brazenness of the thieves, who risked their lives to acquire some property. To exempt the ram rustlers from punishment suggests some justification for their crime. Is their boldness bred of desperation, making the thieves more deserving of its acquisition than the owner?

In another Talmudic passage, one of the sages upbraids Rabbi Eleazar for turning in thieves to the King, even though he is simply enforcing the law. Rabbi Joshua ben Korcha asks, "How long will you deliver up the people of God for slaughter?" When Rabbi Eleazar replies that he is "merely weeding out thorns from the vineyard," his colleague tells him to leave that job up to God. "Let the Owner of the vineyard come in person and weed out the thorns!"

If Rabbi Joshua believes theft a serious crime, why doesn't he laud Rabbi Eleazar's efforts? Even though God is the ultimate guarantor of the moral order, we are often instructed to act as God's agents. Would Rabbi Joshua feel differently if his colleague was nabbing thieves for a Jewish court instead of the Roman king? Or were the thieves stealing from the Romans, which, Rabbi Joshua may believe, they deserved?

The Rabbis' apparent ambivalence about the prohibition against stealing is rooted in another profound Jewish value. In Leviticus (25:23), God announces, "The Land is Mine — you are but temporary settlers on it." Suddenly private property seems moot, and Torah lays out for us directions for distributing God's bounty. The corners of the field belong to the poor, as do the sheaves fallen from the arms of the harvesters, and fruit left unpicked by the pruners. Do we own our land or not? Are we even the temporary owners, if others have a right to the corners (which must be at least 1/60 of the field), to the produce that has fallen to the ground and, in the most extreme example (Deuteronomy 23:35), to as much as they can eat? Even our claim to stewardship is dependent on upholding Divine standards for sharing our blessings. The absolute prohibition against theft is weakened when we fail.

A tale in the Talmud begins to flesh out this tension. Rav Huna's wine starts to turn to vinegar, and the sages wonder whether this is related to some sin on his part. They hear that the great teacher refused to give his tenant his lawful share of vine shoots, but Rav Huna claims that the tenant stole all the shoots, leaving none for Rav Huna to give to him. The sages quote a proverb: "Even if you steal what is yours from a thief, you are still a bit of a thief yourself," suggesting that the tenant took matters into his own hands only to right the wrong of Huna's withholding shoots. Rav Huna pledges to give the tenant his proper share — and the selling price of vinegar in the community soars as high as wine, rewarding Rav Huna for his act of *teshuvah*. Although we are dealing here with two thieves, the greater sinner seems to be Rav Huna, who has the power to prevent the tenant's theft by giving him his share to begin with. The sense that thievery may be prevented by adhering to the laws of sharing property makes the owner (particularly a sage who should be a model of *tzedakah*) more culpable than the tenant, and a more complex view of ownership emerges.

Theft is wrong, *a priori,* because it takes from others and it takes from God, who has ordained a method for distributing Divine bounty. The Holy One apportions the land and wealth that belong to God to individuals who are commanded to share it with God's agents, the poor. The responsibility of the poor is to gather their portion — the corners of the fields and the gleanings from fruit trees, vines, and grain. (When vines fall from the hired gatherers' arms, it is as though God causes them to fall, as though God accompanies the harvesters and harvests for the poor.) Corners are an ambiguous part of the owner's field, the place where it comes together with and reveals the vast expanse of God's property; the owner must share the corner with God.

Theft is ambiguous only when a person is driven to it because God's agents have been lax in their duty to share the Divine bounty given them. Theft ranks with murder because it may deprive people of their livelihood, but if you are the one depriving a person of a livelihood, even by legal means, you are the one to be punished. You are "a bit of a thief" yourself. The thief, the miser, and the exploiter all steal from God.

We may ask: If God is so concerned about the poor as to make them agents in the distribution of Divine property, why does God permit poverty in the first place? The Torah makes it clear that God does not want there to be poverty: "For there shall be no needy among you" (Deuteronomy 15:4), and yet because people will not allow themselves to be naturally generous, God knows "the needy shall not cease from the midst of the land" (Deuteronomy 15:11). For this reason the Holy One gave us *mitzvot* to overcome our natural selfishness. Poor people are living, painful evidence of our lack of generosity, a reminder of the gap between what we are and what God wants us to be — indeed, how God created us before the *yetser hara* (evil inclination) of material desires corrupted us. In the faces of the poor, we can see the face of a judging God. To steal from the poor, therefore, is to diminish the face of God, just as murder destroys the image of God.

Does this principle apply also to stealing in the non-material realm? Does God also own reputations, time, knowledge, and ideas — and do we have an obligation to share them as well as respect them?

To ask the question is to answer it. We can easily expand the teaching cited above to read: Let the (intellectual) property of everyone, the reputation of everyone, the time of everyone, be as precious to you as your own. A reputation once damaged is very difficult to restore; time stolen is irreplaceable. Gossip, flattery, keeping people waiting, failing to give credit for borrowed ideas — these are challenges to God's gift of time, to God's nurturing of self-esteem, and to the Divine creativity that God shares with flesh and blood.

Here too, the "haves" are obliged to give to the "have-nots," and the principles of stewardship apply. Ideas, intellectual property, are meant to be shared and the "payment" is giving proper credit. Those with a strong sense of self should build the esteem of others. "Creators" of some ideas need be modest enough to admit that their ideas really deserve to be in the public domain.

If we abuse our own reputation with unworthy actions, we ought not be surprised if gossip weakens our claim to a good name.

Thou shalt not steal, but if we are robbed by the poor, or if our not-so-original ideas are borrowed, or if our own questionable actions are gossiped about, we need to judge ourselves as harshly as we would judge the thieves, the plagiarists, or the gossips. Stealing is a serious crime in Jewish tradition. So is the sin of encouraging stealing by refusing to share the bounty God has temporarily entrusted to us.

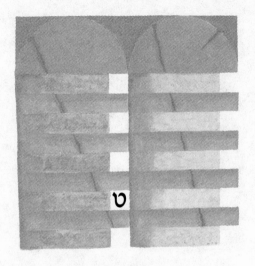

nine

לא תענה ברעך

עד שקר.

You shall not answer against your neighbor
as a false witness.

The Ninth Commandment

False witness, not false testimony

The Torah focuses on a false witness *(eid)* rather than on false testimony *(eidut)*. Even if the testimony is factually true, it is false if the witness did not see it. Maimonides rules that even if you hear from many great and pious people that someone committed a crime or borrowed money, you may not testify regarding the event. Hearsay evidence is unacceptable no matter how unimpeachable the source. *Lo ta'aneh* — if you answer or repeat what you do not know to be true, you are a false witness.

Keep far from a false matter

If your friend or teacher says, "You know I would not lie, even for a large amount of money. Someone owes me money, but I have only one witness against him," you may not testify on his behalf. You cannot even go and stand with your friend or teacher in court, lest it give the impression that there are two witnesses, pressuring the debtor to confess. Even though you do not lie, the Torah commands: *Keep far from a false matter* (Exodus 23:7).

Ma'aseh shehayah... It once happened

that Leo Frank, a Jew raised in Brooklyn, found himself managing his uncle's pencil factory in Atlanta, Georgia. When a fourteen-year-old employee, Mary Phagan, was found murdered in the factory basement in 1913, Frank was arrested for the crime. The key witness for the prosecution was himself suspected of the murder, and there was no real evidence against Frank, but he was convicted and sentenced to death. While many observers remained unconvinced of his guilt, local sentiment ran against this highly educated Northern Jew, and all legal appeals were denied. After the persistent pleas of Frank's wife Lucille, the governor commuted the sentence to life in prison. It cost Governor Slaton his political career, but that still could not save Leo Frank's life. On August 16, 1915, a mob broke into the jail and lynched him.

While only one man committed perjury, many others advanced the false testimony with their own prejudice.

Many weapons of the mouth

The essence of this pronouncement is against perjury, but it also teaches us how many ways we can cause injury with the words we speak: Mockery, slander, denigration, public insults, self-righteous reproof, are all forbidden. They take from people what is not ours to take — self-esteem, reputation — and the offense is compared to theft. When shame results, blood drains from their faces and the Rabbis see a parallel with murder. By these extraordinary comparisons, the Talmud makes clear how grave the sins of speech can be.

The strict standards for speech in Jewish tradition are extremely difficult to obey. The Rabbis of the Talmud understand our limited control over our tongue and imagine God crying out: What should be done with you, deceitful tongue? The other parts of the human body are standing erect, and you are lying down. The other parts are on the outside and you are guarded inside, surrounded by two walls — one of bone and one of flesh — and still you unleash such destruction!

Slander

In the United States, we understand that slander is immoral, because it is false. In Hebrew, slander is called *motzi shem ra,* "drawing out a bad reputation," and the Rabbis delight in thinking that it is no accident that it sounds like *metzora,* "leprosy," because the real defect is in those who say it and spread it.

Lashon hara (the evil tongue), however, is by definition true! It is immoral because it lowers esteem. We are also prohibited from *avak lashon hara,* literally "the dust of the evil tongue": prohibited from the faces, tones, and innuendo that are used to tear people down just as surely as speech itself.

Gossip

The evil tongue comes in many forms. One is gossip *(rechilut),* the idle chatter about other people that cannot possibly be as interesting as we think it is. Our egos are so fragile that, sometimes, other people's strengths make us feel weak and we have to cut them down to size. Other people's weaknesses make us forgive our own; talking about them relieves the moral pressure. Criticizing them increases our own sense of power. Or, as Samuel Johnson said, we share secrets because the vanity of being trusted with a secret is generally the chief motive to disclose it.

Sinful reproof

Even constructive criticism runs the risk of becoming sinful speech. In Leviticus, it is written, "You shall surely reprove your neighbor, but incur no guilt because of him" (Leviticus 19:17). There are two parts to this verse: Once we accept that protest is an imperative of piety (even over against God!), we have to recognize that piety demands training in the art of protest. We must not sin in our criticizing other people.

Maimonides teaches in the *Mishneh Torah:* He who rebukes another, whether for offenses against the rebuker or for sins against God, should administer the rebuke in private, speak to the offender gently and tenderly, and...speak only for the wrongdoer's own good. Obviously, then (but not so obvious to most people today), the criticism must be taken up directly with the offender. If we do not have the courage to do so, the reproof must remain unspoken. If we cannot say it to their face, we cannot say it. It should also remain unspoken if we may be protesting as a righteous facade, for personal gain or emotional retribution. We are required to conduct a thorough exam of our motives, and repent of our own sins before we open our mouths. If it does not pain us to reprove our neighbor, our motives are not pure. Love without criticism is not love, says the *midrash.* But criticism without love is a sin.

Why do we lie?

Everything in the world was created by God except the art of lying.

— *Rachel S. Mikva*

Competing Values

LAURA GELLER

Not long ago, a family came to see me to help them deal with a problem. The mother and stepfather sat down close together at the table in my study, and the teenage son deliberately sat across from them. His arms were folded defiantly across his chest; it was obvious he didn't want to be there. The mother fought back tears as she admitted that her son had been caught lying. The particular circumstances don't really matter; it wasn't the first time he had lied. It was just the most serious. The teenager shrugged as he played with his hair: "Rabbi, what's the big deal? All grownups lie. My parents lie." The mother became indignant, her dark eyes flashing with exasperation and hurt. "That's not true! I never lie!"

Her son shot back: "You lied when you told me that you and Daddy would never get divorced!" She stopped for a minute, tears welling in her eyes. Finally she quietly responded: "When I said that, I believed it was true. I didn't think we would ever get divorced. But certain things happened that changed the situation. It wasn't a lie."

Desperately she turned to me: "Rabbi, tell him that lying is wrong. It's one of the Ten Commandments, isn't it?"

Actually, a prohibition against *all* lying isn't one of the Ten Commandments. There is instead a prohibition against a specific kind of lying: The ninth commandment says, "You shall not answer against your neighbor as a false witness." In Exodus, the term for false witness is *eid sheker;* in Deuteronomy, it is *eid shav.* The adjective *sheker* is usually translated as "fraudulent" or "wrongfully injurious." The adjective *shav* is usually translated as "empty," "in vain," or "lying." Most commentaries see the phrases as synonymous. While some interpretations connect the prohibition to various kinds of injurious speech like gossip, libel, or lying in a business transaction, most hold this commandment to relate to false testimony in court.

The seriousness of bearing false witness in a court of law is obvious: An innocent person could be found guilty. If one has been found guilty of giving false testimony, the Torah enjoins (in Deuteronomy 19:19): "You shall do to him as he schemed to do to his fellow." According to Maimonides, "If their testimony was calculated to occasion a monetary loss, we are to inflict upon them an equal loss; if it was calculated to cause death, they are to suffer the same kind of death."

To protect against false testimony, Jewish tradition is very specific about who can be a witness, and how witnesses are to be examined. It is also clear that at least two witnesses are generally necessary in order to secure a conviction. Great care is taken to insure that the accused will be granted a fair trial.

It is, therefore, never acceptable to lie in a court of law. But the ninth commandment doesn't tell us about other kinds of lies. Is lying ever permissible? When are we obligated to tell the truth? What about withholding the truth? Is that the same as lying?

These questions seem be the subtext of so many front-page news stories. Presidents lie. Politicians claim they didn't know contributions were illegal. Scientific research is stolen or faked. Statements in court and in the press can no longer be assumed to be true. Tobacco companies argue they didn't know that nicotine was addictive. The list goes on and on. No wonder that teenage boy was confused about lying.

What does Jewish tradition teach us about telling the truth and about lying? At first glance, the Torah seems to be quite clear. There are several unconditional prohibitions in Torah such as: "Keep far from a false matter" (Exodus 23:7) and "Neither shall you deal falsely nor lie to one another" (Leviticus 19:11). The

Talmud also seems to support the view that truth-telling is a basic obligation: "One must not speak one thing with the mouth and another with the heart."

Clearly, Judaism believes that we are fundamentally obligated to tell the truth. We must have a basic trust that people tell the truth; without this trust, communication between people is impossible and institutions collapse.

While trust in the words of others is clearly necessary for social relations, does this mean that it is never permissible to lie? Is there ever justification for lying? Are all lies the same? What do we say to the teenager who says: "All adults lie?" Is it always a *mitzvah* to tell the truth?

Philosophers and theologians have wrestled with this question for centuries. From St. Augustine to Thomas Aquinas to Immanuel Kant, they have taken positions ranging from ruling out all lying to distinguishing among kinds of lies. Aquinas would have answered this teenager with "Yes, all adults do lie, but some lies are a mortal sin. Which kind was yours?" Other philosophers allow us to say something misleading while qualifying the statement mentally to make it true. This kind of argument might justify the teenager who lies to his parents about whether his friends take drugs: "No, mom, there were no drugs at the party," he says, thinking, "I mean, no serious drugs like heroin or crack. Only marijuana." Others argue that a falsehood is not a lie unless the person to whom it is addressed has a right to know the truth. A robber has no right to know where a safe is located. Our teenager might think, "It's none of your business anyway. It's my life. You have no right to know, so I am not lying when I don't respond to you truthfully."

All these strategies were rejected by the eighteenth-century philosopher Immanuel Kant who argued that it is never permissible to lie. For him the duty of truthfulness is an "unconditional duty which holds in all circumstances." Even if a lie does not harm any particular individual, it always harms society because "it vitiates the source of law." In addition, a lie harms the liar by destroying his dignity. For Kant, there can be no circumstance when lying is permissible, even if the lie would save a life. He argues that if you tell the truth, even to murderers who ask if their intended victims are in your house, you are not responsible for the murders. If, on the other hand, you tell a lie, you are responsible for anything bad that might happen to the victims or anyone else, as in the case where the victims were not hiding in the place you thought but instead in the place your lie led the murderers. For Kant, there are no excuses for our teenager.

Jewish tradition takes a very different position, one that is more nuanced and textured. Consider the classic text, found in the Talmud. It asks: "What words does one say to a bride? The School of Shammai says: 'The bride is described as she is.' The School of Hillel says: 'Every bride is described as beautiful and graceful.'" The Rabbis agree with Hillel.

But if the bride is ugly, Hillel is lying, isn't he? Perhaps telling an unattractive bride she is beautiful isn't really lying; it is simply making an ambiguous statement. While she might not be physically beautiful, the bride is (most likely, anyway) a beautiful person inside! Or maybe telling her she is beautiful is a simple convention of speech, as when we say: "What a beautiful baby" even if the baby is rather plain. Or we respond to "How are you?" with "Fine, thank you," even if we are not really fine. Because we understand that these words are not meant to be taken literally, we are not lying. The Rabbis describe this as *devarim shebalev,* words in the heart or white lies.

Even God tells white lies, according to the Talmud: "At the School of Rabbi Ishmael it was taught: Great is the cause of peace, seeing that for its sake even the Holy One modified a statement. For at first it is written, 'My Lord being old,' and afterwards it is written, 'And I am old.'"

The *midrash* refers to the story of Abraham and Sarah learning that they will have a son in their old age. When Sarah hears this, she laughs and says, "After I am grown old shall I have pleasure, my lord [Abraham] being old too?" When God confronts Abraham asking, "Why did Sarah laugh?" God reports to Abraham that she had said, "How can I bear a child when I am old?" but God neglects to mention to Abraham that Sarah had also said that Abraham was too old as well. Why does God leave out the part that might hurt Abraham's feelings? Rashi's response is clear: For the sake of peace between husband and wife, *shalom bayit,* lying is acceptable. Other commentators disagree with Rashi. They have trouble imagining God lying outright, even a white lie for the sake of peace. They take a different position, arguing that in this case there was no outright lie, just a minor omission. God might omit a few details, but God doesn't lie.

In a classic *midrash,* we learn more about the value of peacemaking, even if it requires lying:

> If two persons had quarreled with each other,
> Aaron would go and sit with one of them and
> say to him: "Son, do you know how your friend
> is taking it? His heart is breaking; he is tearing
> his garments and saying, 'Woe is me! How can I
> look my friend in the face? I am ashamed on his
> account because it was I who misbehaved
> towards him!'" Aaron would sit with him until he
> dispelled the resentment from his heart. Then
> Aaron would go and sit with the other one and
> say to him: "Son, do you know how your friend
> is taking it? His heart is breaking; he is tearing
> his garments and saying, 'Woe is me! How can I
> look my friend in the face? I am ashamed on his
> account because it was I who misbehaved
> towards him!'" Aaron would sit with him until he
> dispelled the resentment from his heart. And
> when they met, they embraced and kissed each
> other. This is why "they wept for Aaron thirty
> days, even all the house of Israel." (Numbers
> 20:29) Whereas with regard to Moses, who
> rebuked them with harsh words, it is stated:
> "and the children of Israel wept for Moses."
> (Deuteronomy 34:8)

Aaron, through manipulating the truth for the sake of peace, was, according to this text, mourned with greater intensity than even Moses — who spoke the harsh and unpleasant truths.

In addition to peace, there are other circumstances when not speaking the truth is permissible. In the Talmud, Rabbi Yehuda teaches that one may refrain from telling the truth in matters related to learning, marriage, and hospitality. When a scholar is asked directly if he has learned a particular tractate of Talmud, he may answer "no" out of a sense of humility even if he has in fact learned it. We may refuse to answer questions about our sex life for the sake of modesty, or decide not to give information about someone's hospitality in order to protect them from unwanted guests.

So out of the specific examples of family life and interpersonal relations described in these texts, we learn that certain values seem to be more urgent than truth-telling: peace in the home, making peace between people, humility, modesty, and protecting a person from being taken advantage of by others. It follows logically, then, that saving a life, which is clearly more important than these other values, would also take precedence over telling the truth. This point is made in the Talmud in connection to the story of Joseph. Joseph's brothers, afraid that Joseph will take revenge against them after their father dies, lie when they say that their father told them to tell Joseph to forgive them. This story suggests that lying to save lives is acceptable, a position totally consonant with the prevailing rabbinic notion that the saving of a life (pikuach nefesh) takes precedent over all but three commandments — committing idolatry, adultery, and murder.

So what do we say to our teenager? Yes, many adults do lie. And sometimes those lies are permissible. But that's not the end of the conversation. Our tradition always asks another question: What effect do these lies have on the liars?

I looked at the angry teenager in my office. His parents clearly no longer trusted him. Lying has consequences, when you get caught — and even if you don't get caught. If this young man really believes that everyone lies, can he trust his friends? How does lying to his parents make him feel inside? Will his own deception lead him to be wary in his relationships? Lying has consequences for the liar.

And what about the mother? Did she lie to her son when she told him that she and his father would never divorce? Not if we understand lying to be speech with the intention to deceive. But perhaps, as parents, we have to be more careful with what we say to our children. As the Talmud instructs us: "One should not promise to give a child something and then not give it to him, because as a result the child will learn to lie."

Adults do lie, sometimes. And sometimes, according to our tradition, it is permissible to lie. Whether it's a simple white lie for the
sake of peace-making or a heart-stopping lie to save another person's life, as when righteous gentiles lied to German soldiers about
hidden Jews, what makes the lie acceptable is that the goal is clear:
to protect the life or the feelings of a human being. The victim of
the lie was not hurt by it; in fact, you can argue that the deceived
was better off for the deception.

But even in these permitted cases, in these cases where it is clear
that lying is the right choice, even here lying has a cost to the liar
and to others, including children. We tell our children: If you are
home alone and someone calls, tell them Mommy's busy and can't
come to the phone. It's a necessary lie, but even that kind of lie has
consequences: Your children notice that you are lying and that you
are also asking them to lie.

If white lies or lies told to avoid hurting people have consequences,
imagine the consequences of other kinds of lies, the kind the tradition won't permit. These lies not only have consequences for the
deceived and the liar, but for society as well. When societal trust is
damaged, the community as a whole is the victim. Political scandals
have robbed voters of a sense of their own importance, and confi-
dence in government is at a very low ebb. Why even bother to vote
if all politicians are the same — and you can't trust them anyway? Lies
by the tobacco companies make us cynical about all big business.
Revelations about journalists who fabricate their stories make it hard
to believe what we read. Increasingly, people feel they can't trust their
doctors, lawyers, accountants, or even clergy. So whom can you trust,
and how do we negotiate in a society so filled with cynicism that
comes from deception? Lying always has consequences.

Yes, we live in a world of competing values: Truth sometimes
conflicts with peace, sensitivity or even safety. But that is too easy
an answer for our teenager and for ourselves. We need to acknowledge our responsibility for the choices we make, including the
choice to lie. We need to ask ourselves: What motivates the lie, a
conflicting moral value or simply the desire to protect our own
selfish interests? Does the lie protect or hurt? Are there unintended
victims of the lie? And what are the consequences to the deceived,
to the liar, and to the rest of us?

So when is lying acceptable? Perhaps the best litmus test is the one described in Sisela Bok's book *Lying:* "First one needs to say — what I am about to do is to tell a lie — and then ask, if the situation were reversed, would I want the lie I am about to tell to be told to me?" We would ask our teenager: Would you have wanted your parents to lie to you as you lied to them?

Of course, the irony of this litmus test is obvious: The liar must first of all be honest with himself.

According to the Talmud, the first question that we will be asked in the World to Come is "Were you honest in your world?" The question challenges us on many different levels. Were you honest in your dealings with other people, in your public life, in your private life, with your family, with your friends? And it also pushes us to ask an even harder question: Were you honest with yourself?

ten

לא תחמד בית רעך.

לא תחמד אשת רעך

ועבדו ואמתו ושורו וחמרו

וכל אשר לרעך.

You shall not covet your neighbor's house.
You shall not covet your neighbor's wife,
or his male or female slave, or his ox or his ass,
or anything that is your neighbor's.

The Tenth Commandment

Is it possible to love someone so that we do not covet their success?

Rabbi Joseph bar Hani says: A man envies everyone except his son and his disciple. We see how sons are exempt in the model of David and Solomon. The old king is not troubled by the courtiers' wish that his son, Solomon, be even more successful than he (I Kings 1:47). We see how disciples are exempt in the model of Elijah and Elisha. When Elisha asks for a double-portion of his master's spirit, Elijah responds that it may be difficult to achieve such prophetic heights, but he has no objection to the goal (II Kings 2:9). Also, Moses seems to be perfectly willing to pass on the mantle of leadership to Joshua. Although Moses is instructed to lay his *hand* upon him in transmitting his spirit and authority, he lays *both* hands upon his faithful disciple (Numbers 27:18, 23).

Moses seems content to pass the leadership responsibilities on to Joshua, but the Rabbis imagine that, as death draws near, he resists. They put dozens of arguments into his mouth to talk the Almighty out of ending his life before entering the Land of Israel. In one *midrash*, Moses finally accepts the Divine decree after standing with Joshua in the Tent of Meeting. As the pillar of cloud descends, Joshua is in communication with God. "What did the Lord say to you?" Moses asks.

Joshua replies, "When the word was revealed to you, did I know what was said?" It is more than Moses can bear. "I'd rather die one hundred deaths than suffer a single pang of envy. Master of Universes, until now I sought life. Now I surrender my soul to You." As it is written in the Songs of Songs: *Love is as strong as death, jealousy as cruel as the grave.* The love is the love of Moses for Joshua, but the jealousy strikes deep in Moses' heart.

Is desire the measure of all things?

Abraham Joshua Heschel asks this question, wondering if even our religious beliefs and moral standards are simply projections of our own desires. He answers his own query by pointing to our disgust at unbridled greed and self-absorption. "Why must a civilization glittering with fortunes and vested interests run out in nausea? Why does the mind decay when the roots of values begin to rot? What is wrong with living in a jungle of incitements? With living in voracity?" We have some divine compulsion to channel our desire to serve higher purposes and achieve "spiritual dignity," not through elimination of the self, but through self-transcendence and wholeheartedness.

The Rabbis of the Talmud also address the tension between the positive and negative aspects of our desire. They imagine that they are able to capture the *yetser hara,* the evil inclination, that exists in conflict with the more righteous instincts *(yetser tov)* in each one of us. Along with the desirable results, however, come some unexpected consequences: No chicken lays an egg and no person builds a house. Our desires for physical pleasure and self-advancement can become destructive if they overwhelm us, but desire itself is essential to our being. So that we may build and strive, the Rabbis release the evil inclination. Like Heschel, the Talmud directs us to channel our desires (even our *yetser hara*) to serve God's purpose.

How do we train our hearts?

If this tenth commandment leads us from the outer world of speech and deeds into our hearts, how do we live up to the charge?

- If we love God with all our heart, as commanded in Deuteronomy (6:5), there will be no room left to desire material things.
- We are commanded to discipline our hearts to accept what is ours and what cannot be ours (objects and abilities). To covet is to deny our own life and our own being, which God cannot abide. Further, we are to condition our minds so that we get repulsed by coveting, and the object becomes less desirable.
- Who is wise? Those who learn from every person. Who is mighty? Those who can master their own passions. Who is rich? Those who rejoice in their portion.

Covet and desire

Covetousness *(chemdah)* is the physical experience of something that is pleasant to the eye. The word in Deuteronomy, desire *(ta'avah),* is yearning for something even though it is not present or not outwardly beautiful.

Ma'aseh shehayah... It once happened

that Naboth the Jezreelite had a vineyard near the palace of Ahab, king of Samaria. Ahab spoke to Naboth, saying, "Give me your vineyard, that I may have it for a vegetable garden, since it is right next to my palace. I will give you a better vineyard in exchange; or, if you prefer, I will give you its worth in money."

Naboth replied, "The Lord forbids that I should give the inheritance of my fathers to you." Ahab came home sullen and dispirited because of Naboth's answer. He lay down upon his bed, turned away his face, and would not eat.

Jezebel, his wife, came to him and said, "Why is your spirit so sad, that you will not eat?" When he explained the situation, she said, "Do you not govern the kingdom of Israel? Arise and eat something, and let your heart be merry; I will give you the vineyard of Naboth the Jezreelite."

She wrote letters in Ahab's name, sealed them with his seal, and sent them to the elders and to the nobles of Naboth's city. She wrote in the letters: Proclaim a fast, and set Naboth at the head of the people. Set two worthless men before him, to bear witness against him, saying, "You blaspheme against God and the king." Then carry him out and stone him to death.

The men of his city, the elders, and nobles did as Jezebel instructed, sending word to the queen that Naboth had been stoned to death. When Jezebel heard that Naboth was dead, she said to Ahab, "Arise, take possession of Naboth's vineyard, which he refused to sell you, for Naboth is dead." Ahab took it.

The prophet Elijah condemned him for his mad covetousness: "Thus says the Lord, 'Would you murder and take possession? In the very place where the dogs lapped up Naboth's blood, the dogs will lap up your blood too.'" (I Kings 21)

— *Rachel S. Mikva*

Desire

MENACHEM KELLNER

Coveting itself is not an action, but rather a frame of mind. How can we be commanded or prohibited with respect to frames of mind? They are not ordinarily thought to be under our control. It is hardly fair to prohibit a person from doing that which he cannot help doing. The other commandments in the Decalogue, not to mention in the Torah generally, are ordinarily understood as referring to action.

Honoring our parents, for example, is presented as involving obligatory, permissible, and impermissible *actions,* not feelings toward our parents. It is possible to dislike or disdain parents (possible, not recommended!) without violating the fifth commandment. But in the tenth commandment, it seems that Torah outlaws an emotion. If feeling can be legislated, why not outlaw hatred, spite, or anger? What is wrong with desire?

Maimonides teaches that the text in Exodus does not forbid us to covet; it forbids us to act out of covetousness. He writes in his *Book of Commandments:* We are forbidden to occupy our minds with schemes to acquire what belongs to another of our brethren. The prohibition, *You shall not covet your neighbor's house,* applies only to putting the desire into practice. The action, however, may seem as innocuous as pestering someone until he sells us the object of our desire.

> If one covets the male slave or the female slave
> or the house or goods of another, or anything
> that it is possible for him to acquire from the
> other, and he subjects the other to vexation and
> pesters him until he is allowed to buy it from
> him, then he transgresses the negative com-

mandment, *You shall not covet,* even if he pays
him a high price for it. *(Maimonides, Mishneh
Torah, Laws of Robbery and Lost Property 1.9)*

Strangely, even pestering and scheming by themselves do not
constitute the violation. The person Maimonides describes does
not sin until he succeeds in acquiring the object that he covets.

In the rabbinic imagination, one transgression leads to another.
Something acquired in violation of religious principles will com-
pound the wages of sin. In the *Mechilta,* a collection of *midrashim* on
the Book of Exodus compiled in the Land of Israel around the
fourth century, the Rabbis perhaps take this concept to the extreme.
They speculate that there is a treacherous connection between coveting and the last commandment on the facing tablet: to honor our
parents. A man who covets his neighbor's wife may, in the end,
commit adultery with her. And she may bear a son who does not
know his biological father (to whom the obligation of filial respect
is owed, according to the halachah). This son will grow up giving
filial respect to one who is not his actual father, and may even be
led to curse (for whatever reason) the man to whom he actually
owes such respect — a capital crime. Although this somewhat fanciful chain of events is far more heinous than the actions
Maimonides mentions, both interpretations are concerned about
the deleterious *results* of coveting. The question remains: Is there
anything sinful about desire itself?

It would seem so. When Moses repeats the "Ten
Commandments" in Deuteronomy, he uses a different word:
desire *(titaveh)* instead of covet *(tachmod).* And so, even though it is
morally problematic to legislate feeling, Maimonides presents the
Deuteronomic version of the *mitzvah* as explicitly prohibiting
thoughts and emotions. He clearly states that even if we only
desire that which belongs to our neighbor, we violate a negative
commandment:

If one desires another's house or his wife or his
goods or any similar thing that he might buy
from him, he transgresses a negative commandment as soon as he thinks in his heart how he is
to acquire the desired object and allows his mind
to be seduced by it. For Scripture says, *Nor shall*

you desire, and desire is a matter of the heart only. *(Mishneh Torah, Laws of Robbery and Lost Property 1.10)*

What is wrong with simply thinking about it? At times, Maimonides is still preoccupied with what actions desire may effect and, in one text, his progression of sins is as dramatic as the sequence of "events" in the *Mechilta.* In the next paragraph of the *Mishneh Torah,* Maimonides teaches:

Desire leads to coveting, and coveting to robbery, for if the owner does not wish to sell, even when he is offered a high price and is greatly impor-tuned, it will lead the coveter to rob him. Moreover, if the owner should stand up to him to protect his property and prevent the robbery, this may lead to bloodshed.

Is he exaggerating? When Jacob desires the birthright, he resorts to extortion, withholding a bowl of stew from his brother until Esau yields. To secure the blessing of the firstborn, he follows his mother's directions to impersonate Esau and deceive his father. Desire leads to coveting; coveting leads to robbery.

When King David desires Bathsheba, he does not only commit adultery. When she becomes pregnant, it seems that his sin will soon be discovered, so the misguided king sends Bathsheba's husband, Uriah, to the battle front to die. Desire leads to coveting, coveting leads to taking, and taking leads to bloodshed.

The prohibition against such powerful desire is not simply to pre-vent the escalation of misdeeds, however. We see how desperately Leah covets the place her sister, Rachel, holds in their husband's heart, and still she does not steal or kill to gain it. Rachel certainly covets her sister's fruitfulness and yet commits no more grievous sin as a consequence. We watch the desire eat at their hearts, however; they seem doomed to live lives of estrangement and quiet desperation, unable to recognize the blessings that are theirs. These unhappy mod-els demonstrate the progressively destructive power of coveting in all its forms. Our own experience with desire may never have led to bloodshed, but it surely has consequences.

Western culture seems to depend on covetousness to drive its economy. Advertisements are designed to inculcate the desire to have something we do not currently own, even if we do not need it. The materialistic society shapes our longings to be competitive and continuous, to acquire what others have. It views desire within the law to be all good and, while it surely recognizes the power of our wants, it denies their insidious tendency to deprive us of balance and contentment.

Desire is predatory; it eats at our own hearts. In its place, God seeks to seal the passion of the covenant to make our hearts whole.

Jewish tradition expresses the commandment against coveting in two different ways in order to guarantee that we understand it not only in legalistic and behavioral terms, but also in terms of the sort of character the Torah is trying to inculcate in us. The Torah does not want us to steal. Fine. But more than that, the Torah wants us to makes ourselves into the kind of people who are not even *tempted* to steal. Thus, we are forbidden to steal, and forbidden to allow ourselves to get into a situation where we might be tempted to steal. We are furthermore bidden to train ourselves not to think about the possessions of others, lest we get ourselves into a situation where we might be tempted to steal.

A "holy nation" is not only a law-abiding nation; it is a nation that has internalized the values inherent in the laws. The tenth commandment thus teaches us that while *mitzvot* are a way of life, they are not ends in themselves, but means to a further end: the formation of a holy character.

This task is not an easy one. As Bahya ibn Pakuda points out in his ethical-religious work (eleventh century), *Duties of the Heart,* it is easier to obey "duties of the limbs," those obligations and prohibitions that involve outward behavior, and which thus involve social approbation and disapprobation, than it is to fulfill the "duties of the heart," since "only" God knows if we have fulfilled the latter, not our neighbors or, often, not even ourselves.

If we succeed in making ourselves into the kind of person who does not covet another's belongings, then the first nine of the Ten Commandments may be said to have done their work. We have internalized their teachings and made ourselves over. In this sense, the "tenth commandment" is not the last because it is the least important; it is the last because it leads the way through law to holiness.

Ten More Words

ARNOLD JACOB WOLF

It is much harder to write about crucial, famous texts than about more obscure and apparently less persuasive ones. What, after all, is left to be said about the Ten Words that has not been said a thousand times? But these essays, while not outlandish or bizarre, bring us new voices and new interpretations.

I am moved not only by the quality of the authors' work (and of their whole lives), but by the diversity represented in this collection. Here, in this one book, are Orthodox and Liberal Jews, Israelis and Americans, men and women, scholars and humble practitioners. I am deeply honored that they have come together to celebrate my modest contributions to Jewish living and learning. Our greatest need these days is to find common ground upon which all Jews can unite, with our differences respected, our common fate acknowledged, and our tradition empowering us all. The personal (though not confessional, in the maudlin current style) as well as the scholarly character of each essay is also enheartening. Torah is not only texts, or perhaps we ourselves are the great texts to be interpreted. We bring to our reading our whole selves. And we bring to our selves the whole body of Torah and millennial tradition.

To my friend of forty years or more, Reb Zalman: You, the most far-ranging and courageous of all of us, still frighten the timid Jew that I am. It is wonderful to see other human-religious alternatives to our own as legitimate and deeply instructive. But crossing all the boundaries and personally experiencing *their* lives with God is idolatry. I am condemned to live — and I choose to live — wholly within my own community and tradition. Most of us are not Zalman. We are too parochial and too afraid. Yet perhaps there is a way this empathic model could be instructive without being dangerous.

To Nancy Fuchs-Kreimer: For me, to honor the name of God is to diminish, even to extinguish my own name. If God is God, then my own reputation, or even my life, is decidedly less important. When I put myself first (as I often do), then I have taken God's primacy in vain: I have made God an adjunct of my own needs or desires. This casts doubt for me on the permissibility or, at least, on the religious status of petitional prayer. Our task is not to beg, but to glorify.

To Lawrence Hoffman, I would ask: Are not the three modes of our understanding (seeking limits, truth, or meaning) not merely consecutive but also dialectical? I hold that limits are still needed and that we have not entirely eschewed the enlightenment search for truth, though we understand it in a new way. I do not think our commandments are merely our way of putting together the varied strands of our disparate lives. I hold that we still need boundaries and standards as well as life-affirming methodologies. You have greatly illumined our options; I choose to accept all of them in concert.

To Leonard Fein: All fathers fail, of course. All of us see in our children's disdain the judgment of Heaven. But we do not *wholly* fail. We mediate the divine love in which we all live and move and have our being. Biology (or its equivalent in the case of adoption) will out. Nature and nurture always prevail. Our children replicate as they supersede ourselves. Most important in my view is the task of commanded honor. Our inevitable ambivalence can only be resolved in action. We are commanded, whatever our mixture of love and hate, of regret and gratitude, to do honor. Doing changes everything.

To my cousin, Levi Weiman-Kelman: I think of you every day — in the land of Israel, loving the land and hating its excesses, loving peace and using your personal power to defend the human rights of Palestinians and other victims. Where we in America fiddle with obscure issues and minor conflicts, you are where the power to kill gives you the power not to kill. Israel is the test of our obedience. If Jews in the Untied States support so many wars (including the recent bombing of the innocent in the name of stopping "ethnic cleansing"), they forget our own version of ethnic cleansing in *Eretz Yisrael*. You, Levi, did not and will not forget.

To Peter Knobel: Marriage recapitulates the covenant between God and ourselves. We can be married only because God has wed us first. Otherwise, marriage would be too difficult. Adultery is the fragmentation of the self, the dissolution of what preserves and protects us as human. Like idolatry, its twin, it destroys the union of self and other, of who we are and whom we love. It sends us all back into chaos.

To Richard Levy: You remind us that everything belongs to God. Is not all property, then, in some sense theft? Are the Marxists right when they seek to expropriate from the expropriators? Or are they merely using the numerical superiority of the proletariat to take what others rightfully own? At least we must admit that many of our gains are ill-gotten, even the ones we are positive we earned. *Genevat da'at* (stealing knowledge) includes the use of our own gifts and abilities against the welfare of others. If we are smarter or richer, we take all the best places in universities and corporations. If we know what the other does not know, we can profit by his or her ignorance. Insider trading is forbidden, even trading in Torah.

To Laura Geller: I am troubled not so much by verbal lies as by a life that is fundamentally inauthentic. If my wife should lie to me (which is almost unthinkable), her "lie" would be more true than many truths I proclaim. Somewhere, somehow, we must surrender our suspicion and come to trust the ones we love. They are the human beings who bear witness to the authenticity of our lives. I can only hope to become more truthful, not only in what I say but in who I am. As witness, we are all (partially) false.

To Menachem Kellner: I suggest my own understanding of the final *mitzvah* in the Ten Words. It is not forbidden to wish to have a house like my neighbor's house or a car like his or even a woman just like his wife. What is forbidden, I think, is to want *his* car or *his* wife, *her* house or *her* husband — to replace the other, not to replicate her. It is all right to want to have a big house. It is forbidden to want to live in someone else's house or life. I am commanded to be me, not you or her. I am forbidden to covet *your* place, to wish to be *you*.

To my beloved brother, Gene Borowitz: As always, you speak for me better than I do myself.

All of you have my love and gratitude, including Lawrence Kushner and Rachel Mikva. I bless God for letting me see this day.

Sources and Notes

Introduction

Page Number

xi *God's utterance at Sinai, though riddled with infinite meaning, is somehow one:* Arthur Green, "The *Aleph-bet* of Creation: Jewish Mysticism for Beginners," *Tikkun* 3:4, p. 45ff.

xii *The second Five commandments were intended to be paired off:* Pesikta Rabati 21:18

xii *The* Zohar *is even more explicit:* II 90a–b

xiii *Along comes the Talmud and, using gematria:* Makot 23b–24a

xiii *As the philosopher Alexander Altman once observed:* "God and the Self in Jewish Mysticism," *Judaism* 3:2 (1954).

xiv *According to a teaching of Rabbi Mendl Torum:* Gershom Scholem, *On the Kabbala and its Symbolism,* translated by Ralph Manheim (New York: Schocken Books, 1965), pp. 29-31.

Perspectives on the Ten Words

xviii *How were the Ten Commandments arranged?:* Mechilta Bachodesh, Chapter 8. Sa'adia Gaon is among those who suggest that all ten are written on both tablets.

xix *Were the Israelites coerced?:* Shabbat 88a, Nedarim 32a

xx *When the Holy One gave the Torah:* Exodus Rabah 29:9

xx *With each and every word of the Holy One:* Shabbat 88b, Zevachim 116a

xx *The Roman emperor Hadrian asked:* Pesikta Rabbati 21

Chapter 1: I, *Adonai* your God, [am the one]

3   *A parable: A new king came to rule:* Mechilta Bachodesh, Chapter 6

3   *Yet Moses Maimonides:* Sefer Hamitzvot, Mitzvot Asei 1; Mishneh Torah, Yesodei HaTorah I:6

4   *In the Talmud, the Rabbis play with gematria:* Makot 23b

4   *Franz Rosenzweig, a modern philosopher:* From his commentary on Yehudah Halevi's poems. See Nahum N. Glatzer, *Franz Rosenzweig: His Life and Thought* (New York: Schocken Books, 1953), p. 285.

4   *All they heard was the first letter:* See Gershom Scholem's discussion in *On the Kabbalah and its Symbolism,* translated by Ralph Manheim (New York: Schocken Books, 1965), pp. 29-31.

4   *It is necessary to identify God as the One:* Mechilta Bachodesh, Chapter 5

6   *As Arthur Green wrote: Seek My Face, Speak My Name* (Northvale, NJ: Jason Aronson, 1992), p. 37.

Chapter 2: Have no other god before Me.

17   *General Agrippa asks Rabban Gamliel:* Avodah Zarah 54b–55a

17   *No matter what kind of face:* Midrash Aseret Hadibrot. See also Rashi's commentary.

17   *Do not make yourself into an idol:* Sanhedrin 61a

18   *How can God hold responsible:* see Sanhedrin 27b, and Ibn Ezra in his Torah commentary.

19   *The secrets within syntax:* Or Hachayim, Umberto Cassuto

19   *Is Judaism then asserting itself as the one "true" religion?:* Adapted from Arnold Jacob Wolf in *Commentary* symposium, "The Condition of Jewish Belief." Published by Macmillan (New York, 1966), p. 270.

19   *Only the names change:* In *Franz Rosenzweig: His Life and Thought,* p. 277.

20   *The gods we worship:* From Ralph Waldo Emerson, as adapted in *Gates of Prayer* (New York: Central Conference of American Rabbis, 1975), p. 240.

21   *Since the day that the Temple was destroyed:* Berachot 8a

22   *Wisdom among the nations — believe it:* Eichah Rabah 2:13

22　　*Several sources suggest that they also had a residue:* See, for example, Eichah Rabah 3:2.

Chapter 3: You shall not lift up the name of *Adonai* your God for vain purpose.

27　　*Jewish tradition distinguishes:* See Sefer Hachinuch.

27　　*The Talmud extends the prohibition to using God's name:* Berachot 33

28　　*We are cautioned not to "carry God's name upon ourselves":* Pesikta Rabati 22

28　　*Rabbi Joseph Soloveitchik teaches that it is a presumption:* See Nehama Leibowitz, *Studies in Shemot* (Jerusalem: World Zionist Organization, 1976), p. 329. Soloveitchik touches on related themes in *The Lonely Man of Faith* (Northvale NJ: Jason Aronson, 1965), pp. 48-49, 101.

29　　*What sort of penalty is this?:* Moshe Chayim Luzzatto, Mesilat Yesharim

33　　*I looked up the origin of the rule in the Talmud:* Berachot 33a

33　　*Shortly after that lunch, I studied a passage in the Talmud:* Yoma 69b

35　　*So much for the Scylla:* Scylla and Charybdis were sea monsters from classical mythology, later identified as a rock and a whirlpool respectively, in the strait of Messina. "Between Scylla and Charybdis" is to stand between two equally perilous alternatives, neither of which can be avoided without encountering and probably falling victim to the other.

35　　*How do we bless God for the evil even as we bless God for the good?:* Berachot 54a

Chapter 4: Remember the Sabbath day and keep it holy.

43　　*All your work?:* Mechilta Bachodesh, Chapter 7

43　　*A palace in time:* Abraham Joshua Heschel, *The Sabbath* (New York: Farrar, Straus and Young, 1951), pp. 3, 10.

44　　*"Keep" and "Remember" in a single utterance:* Mechilta Bachodesh, Chapter 7, Beitsa 16a

44　　*How do we make the Sabbath holy?* Chofetz Chaim

45　　Ma'aseh shehayah... *It once happened:* Shabbat 150a, Sanhedrin 119a

45	*Shabbat as protest:* See also Jeffrey K. Salkin, *Being God's Partner* (Jewish Lights, 1994), pp. 163–168.
46	*The pause between the notes: Likrat Shabbat* (Bridgeport CT: Media Judaica, 1973), p. 99.
48	*The traditional liturgy suggests God's role: Hasidur Hashalem: Daily Prayer Book,* ed. Phillip Birnbaum (New York: Hebrew Publishing Company, 1949; reprinted many times thereafter), pp. 289, 267, 353, 395, 453.
48	*In seventeenth- and eighteenth-century Salonika:* The halachic issue involved is the prohibition against getting around Sabbath work regulations (in this case, making a fire to heat coffee) by arranging for non-Jews to do it. If the coffee just happened to be available, drinking it on the Sabbath would have been acceptable, as long as no money changed hands on the holy day. But in this case, coffeehouse owners were making coffee expressly for Jewish patrons. On the Salonikan Jewish community during this period, see the very fine thesis by Deborah Ellen Zecher, "A Case Study of Jewish Community in Decline, as Reflected by Isaac Molcho in *Orchot Yosher*" (Master's thesis, Hebrew Union College-Jewish Institute of Religion, New York, 1982).
49	*The Sabbath is a day of consecration:* See Michael A. Meyer, *A Response to Modernity: A History of the Reform Movement in Judaism* (New York: Oxford Press, 1988), pp. 387–88.
51	*Help us to preserve the Sabbath: Union Prayer Book* (1895), p. 24.
52	*Steven Goldberg, a professor of Sociology:* "The Erosion of the Social Sciences," in Katharine Washburn and John Thornton, eds., *Dumbing Down: Essays on the Strip Mining of American Culture* (New York: W. W. Norton, 1996), p. 97.
53	*Synagogues should elect to become communities of meaning:* See Lawrence A. Hoffman, "From Common Cold to Uncommon Healing," *CCAR Journal* (Spring, 1994), pp. 1–30.
54	*We might find the answer to our Shabbat question in Langer's view of aesthetics:* Susanne K. Langer, *Feeling And Form* (New York: Charles Scribner and Sons, 1953).
55	*A sanctuary in time:* Abraham Joshua Heschel, *The Sabbath* (New York: Farrar, Straus and Young, 1951).
56	Six Degrees of Separation: by John Guare (New York: Vintage, 1990), p. 81.

Chapter 5: Honor your father and mother that your days may be prolonged....

61   *There are three partners in the making of a human being:* Kiddushin 30b–31a

62   *Honor and fear/revere:* Kiddushin 31

62   *The Talmud suspects that we tend to honor our mother more than our father:* Kiddushin 31b

62   *How far should it go?:* Pesikta Rabati 23, 24; Mechilta Bachodesh, Chapter 8

63   *According to the Talmud, there is a reward:* Kiddushin 39b, Chulin 142a

63   *In Deuteronomy, the phrase is included:* Ha'amek Davar

63   Ma'aseh shehayah... *It once happened:* Kiddushin 31

64   *As Marion Wright Edelman, the head of the Children's Defense Fund writes: The Measure of Our Success* (Boston: Beacon Press, 1993).

65   *The mother of Rabbi Ishmael:* Palestinian Talmud, Pe'ah 1:1, 15c–d

66   Na'ar hayiti vegam zakanti: From *birkat hamazon,* the blessing after the meal.

Chapter 6: You shall not murder.

75   *In the Talmud we learn that if we publicly embarrass someone:* Baba Metsia 58b

75   *If you cause people to lose their livelihood:* Yevamot 78b

75   *Even a host who fails to provide:* Sotah 45b–46a

75   *What about the death penalty?:* Makot 7a

76   *When Rabbi Judah haNasi became deathly ill:* Ketubot 104a

77   *Rabbi Yehuda teaches in the name of Samuel:* Yoma 85b

77   *The case that came before Raba:* Pesachim 25b

77   *The bloods of your brother:* Sanhedrin 4:5

77   *Destroying (or saving) the entire world:* Sanhedrin 37a

77   *The modern philosopher, Emmanuel Levinas:* "Ethics and Spirit," in *Difficult Freedom* (Baltimore: Johns Hopkins University Press, 1990), p. 10.

78   *If it is in our power to protest:* Avodah Zarah 4a

78   *Abraham Joshua Heschel echoes this warning: The Earth is the Lord's* (Woodstock, VT: Jewish Lights Publishing, 1995).

79   *The Torah was revealed not only to the Jews:* Based on *Genesis Rabah 27:40, Sifre Deuteronomy 343, Pesikta Rabati 21.* The rabbinic imagination is taken by a verse in Deuteronomy (33:2), which they read: "The Lord came unto Sinai after [first] having risen at Seir unto the people there, then having shined forth at Mount Paran. [Finally] God came to the holy myriads, and in Gods' right hand — a fiery law for them." With the addition of the words in brackets, the text implies that God offered the Torah to other peoples first. The simple reading of this blessing from Moses at the end of his life describes God's continual presence among the people of Israel.

82   *My brother came back from the field dressed in gray:* Translation by T. Carmi, ed., *The Penguin Book of Hebrew Verse* (New York: Viking Press, 1981), p. 559.

82   *The tongue is compared to an arrow:* Midrash on Proverbs

Chapter 7: You shall not commit adultery.

87   Ma'aseh shehayah... *It once happened:* Leviticus Rabah 9:9

87   *We lose what we have:* Sotah 9a–b

88   *Fidelity is more than skin deep:* Leviticus Rabah 23:12

88   *"You must not commit adultery" is parallel:* Mechilta Bachodesh, Chapter 8

88   *Even if we assist in arranging the rendezvous:* Shevuot 47b

89   *Weakening of love:* Sanhedrin 7a

89   *A consuming fire:* Sotah 17a, Lekach Tov

92   *Time and again the Torah:* Daniel Schiff, *Separating the Adult from Adultery* (unpublished). See pages 34–36.

93   *By the time of the* Mishnah: Sotah 47

93   *As rabbis have increasingly become pastors more than teachers and adjudicators:* The document of ordination still describes the role of rabbi with the definitive charge: "*Yoreh yoreh, yadin yadin.* This one is now fully authorized to teach and to judge."

93   *Eugene Borowitz, in his book:* See *Choosing a Sex Ethic: A Jewish Inquiry* (New York: Schocken, 1969).

95   *Rabbi Arnold Jacob Wolf reminds us:* See *Commentary* symposium, "The Condition of Jewish Belief," p. 270.

Chapter 8: You shall not steal.

99   Ma'aseh shehayah... *It once happened:* While this story can-
        not be found in any of the classic rabbinic sources, the edi-
        tor of this volume can attest to its validity. She is the
        daughter (and later the rabbi) in the tale.

99   *Steal what?:* Mechilta Bachodesh, Chapter 8 identifies kid-
        napping as the primary prohibition. Sforno, in his Torah
        commentary, discusses some of the broader meanings. See
        also Baba Metsia 58b and 62a, Chulin 94a.

100   *Partners to the crime:* Mishneh Torah, Gezeilah vaAveidah
        3:1, 1:1, Geneivah 5:1

100   *When the people of Nineveh seek to repent:* Ta'anit 16a

100   *This extreme is balanced:* See Baba Kama 66b and 95a

100   *The disciples of Rabbi Johanan ben Zakkai:* Baba Kama 79b

104   *Let the property of every human being be as precious to you as
        your own:* Pirkei Avot 2:12

104   *Said Rabbi Yochanan: When people rob even as little as a
        perutah:* Baba Kama 119a

104   *God did not decree punishment for the generation of the Flood
        until:* Sanhedrin 108a

104   *Shmuel said: Even if someone took a single beam:* Ta'anit 16a

104   *If someone has consumed stolen food, the thief can never return it:*
        Chulin 89a

105   *Thieves once broke in and stole some rams:* Sanhedrin 72a

105   *In another Talmudic passage, one of the sages upbraids Rabbi
        Eleazar:* Baba Metsia 83b

106   *Rav Huna's wine starts to turn to vinegar:* Ta'anit 20b

Chapter 9: You shall not answer against your neighbor as a false witness.

111   *False witness, not false testimony:* Mishneh Torah, Eidut 17:13

111   *Keep far from a false matter:* Shevuot 31a

112   *The strict standards for speech:* Arachin 15b

112   *Slander:* Resh Lakish makes the connection between lep-
        rosy and slander in Arachin 15b. The phrase *avak lashon
        hara* can be found there as well, and in Baba Kama 165a.

113   *Once we accept that protest is an imperative of piety:* Orchot
        Tsadikim

113   *Maimonides teaches in the* Mishneh Torah: Hilchot De'ot 6:7

113   *It should also remain unspoken:* Baba Metsia 107b

113   *Love without criticism is not love:* Genesis Rabah 84:3

113   *Why do we lie?:* Pesikta Rabati 24

117   *One must not speak one thing with the mouth and another with the heart:* Baba Metsia 49a

117   *For [Kant] the duty of truthfulness is an unconditional duty:* Immanuel Kant, *Critique of Pure Reason and Other Writings in Moral Philosophy,* ed. Lewis W. Beck (Chicago: University of Chicago Press, 1949) p. 346 ff.

118   *What words does one say to a bride?:* Ketubot 16b-17a

118   *Even God tells white lies:* Yevamot 65b

119   *If two persons had quarreled with each other:* Avot deRabbi Natan

119   *Rabbi Yehuda teaches that one may refrain from telling the truth:* Baba Metsia 23b-24a

120   *Joseph's brothers, afraid that Joseph will take revenge:* Yevamot 65

120   *One should not promise to give a child something and then not give it:* Sukah 46b

122   *First one needs to say:* Sisela Bok, *Lying* (New York: Vintage Books, 1989).

122   *Were you honest in your world?:* Shabbat 113a

For an excellent discussion of Jewish tradition's attitude toward lying, see Mark Dratch, "Nothing But the Truth?" in *Judaism: A Quarterly Journal of Jewish Life and Thought,* Vol. 37 No. 2 (Spring 1988).

Chapter 10: You shall not covet...

125   *Rabbi Joseph bar Hani says:* Sanhedrin 105b

125   *In one* midrash, *Moses finally accepts the Divine decree:* Deuteronomy Rabah 9:9

125   *Abraham Joshua Heschel asks: God in Search of Man* (New York: Farrar, Straus & Giroux, 1955), p. 396

126   *The Rabbis of the Talmud also address the tension:* Yoma 69b

126   *If we love God with all our heart:* Jacob Zvi Mecklenberg, Haketav Vehakabbalah

126   *We are commanded to discipline:* Ibn Ezra

126   *Who is wise?:* Pirkei Avot 4:1

127   *Covet and desire:* Malbim

About the Contributors

EUGENE B. BOROWITZ

Rabbi Eugene B. Borowitz is the Sigmund L. Falk Distinguished Professor of Education and Jewish Religious Thought at the New York School of Hebrew Union College-Jewish Institute of Religion where he has taught since 1962. He is the only person to have received a national Foundation for Jewish Culture Lifetime Achievement Award in Scholarship for work in the field of Jewish Thought. His most recent books are *The Jewish Moral Virtues* (with Frances W. Schwartz) and *Judaism After Modernity*.

LEONARD FEIN

Leonard Fein is a writer, a teacher, and a veteran activist in the work of *tikkun olam*. He is the founder of *Moment* magazine; of Mazon: A Jewish Response to Hunger; and of the National Jewish Coalition for Literacy. Currently, he serves as Director of the Commission on Social Action of Reform Judaism.

NANCY FUCHS-KREIMER

Rabbi Nancy Fuchs-Kreimer is a 1982 graduate of the Reconstructionist Rabbinical College. She holds a Ph.D. from Temple University Religion Department. She has taught contemporary Jewish thought and comparative religion at RRC for 12 years. Currently, she is the Rabbinic Director of the Jewish Identity Program of the Jewish Family and Children's Service of greater Philadelphia. She is the author of *Parenting as a Spiritual Journey: Deepening Ordinary and Extraordinary Events into Sacred Occasions* (Jewish Lights Publishing).

LAURA GELLER

Rabbi Laura Geller is the Senior Rabbi of Temple Emanuel in Beverly Hills, California (1994–). Ordained at Hebrew Union College in 1976, she is the first woman to be selected to lead a major metropolitan synagogue. She served as the Executive Director of the American Jewish Congress Pacific Southwest Region (1990–94), where she helped to create the Feminist Center and the Jewish Urban Affairs Center. From 1976 to 1990 Rabbi Geller served as Director of Hillel at the University of Southern California. Her articles on Jewish feminism have appeared in numerous journals and books, including *Beginning Anew, Four Centuries of Jewish Women's Spirituality, On Being a Jewish Feminist,* and *Gender and Judaism.*

LAWRENCE A. HOFFMAN

Rabbi Lawrence A. Hoffman is Professor of Liturgy at the New York School of the Hebrew Union College-Jewish Institute of Religion, and a co-founder of Synagogue 2000, an institute for the Synagogue of the 21st Century. Among his books are: *Israel — A Spiritual Travel Guide: A Companion for the Modern Jewish Pilgrim* (Jewish Lights Publishing, 1998), *What is a Jew* (Macmillan, 1993), and *The Art of Public Prayer: Not For Clergy Only* (SkyLight Paths Publishing, 1999). He is also general editor of *Minhag Ami: My People's Prayer Book* (Jewish Lights Publishing).

MENACHEM KELLNER

Menachem Kellner is Wolfson Professor of Jewish Thought at the University of Haifa and author, most recently, of *Must a Jew Believe Anything?* (Littman), as well as translator of Levi Ben Gershom's *Commentary on Song of Songs* (Yale).

PETER S. KNOBEL

Rabbi Peter S. Knobel is the Senior Rabbi of Beth Emet The Free Synagogue in Evanston, Illinois. He was ordained by the Hebrew Union College in 1969 and received his Ph.D. at Yale University in 1976. He is currently the Chair of the Liturgy Committee of the Central Conference of American Rabbis. He is past president of both the Chicago Board of Rabbis and the Chicago Association of Reform Rabbis. Rabbi Knobel has published a number of scholarly works on Jewish subjects. He provides much local and national leadership in various Jewish organizations.

LAWRENCE KUSHNER

Rabbi Lawrence Kushner serves at Congregation Beth El in Sudbury, Massachusetts. He is author of many creative religious works, including *Invisible Lines of Connection: Sacred Stories of the Ordinary, The Book of Words: Talking Spiritual Life, Living Spiritual Talk, God Was in This Place and I, i Did Not Know: Finding Self, Spirituality, and Ultimate Meaning,* and *Honey from the Rock: An Easy Introduction to Jewish Mysticism.* His stories and teachings have contributed greatly to contemporary spiritual renewal. Rabbi Kushner's first position after ordination was as a Rabbinic Fellow, working with and learning from Arnold Jacob Wolf at Congregation Solel in Highland Park, Illinois.

RICHARD N. LEVY

Rabbi Richard N. Levy is Director of the School of Rabbinic Studies at the Los Angeles campus of the Hebrew Union College-Jewish Institute of Religion. From 1975 to 1999 he was Executive Director of Los Angeles Hillel Council, a regional center of Hillel: the Foundation for Jewish Campus Life. He came to the Hillel Council at UCLA in 1968, and served until 1975 as its Director. From 1997–1999 Rabbi Levy was President of the Central Conference of American Rabbis (CCAR). He is a gifted teacher and liturgist, doing much of the writing and translating for *On Wings of Awe, On Wings of Freedom,* and *On Wings of Light.* He received the prestigious Covenant Foundation Award for Distinguished Educators in 1994. He and his wife, Carol Levy, have two children, Sarah Miriam and Elizabeth Mauree.

RACHEL S. MIKVA

Rabbi Rachel S. Mikva is rabbi of Community Synagogue in Rye, New York. Ordained at HUC–JIR in 1990, she had the privilege of serving with Rabbi Wolf for four years at K.A.M. Isaiah Israel. She serves on the UAHC–CCAR Commission for Religious Living, as well the Responsa Committee and numerous other community and national not-for-profit boards. Rabbi Mikva was the editor of *Mahshavot, A Journal of the Chicago Board of Rabbis*

147

(1992–1997) and has published articles on a variety of Jewish topics. She is married to Mark Rosenberg, and they have two children: Jacob and Keren.

ZALMAN M. SCHACHTER-SHALOMI

Rabbi Zalman M. Schachter-Shalomi holds the World Wisdom Chair at the Naropa Institute. In 1989 he founded the transdenominational Spiritual Eldering Institute and he is a major figure in the Jewish spiritual renewal movement. Reb Zalman is an eminent rabbi and professor emeritus at Temple University. He is the author of over 150 articles and monographs on Jewish spiritual life and has translated many Chasidic and Kabbalistic texts. His most recent books include *Spiritual Intimacy, Gate to the Heart, and Spiritual Eldering: From Age-ing to Sage-ing.*

LEVI WEIMAN-KELMAN

Rabbi Levi Weiman-Kelman is the founding rabbi of Congregation Kol Haneshama in Jerusalem. He teaches liturgy at HUC–JIR in Israel and serves as chairperson of *Shomrei Mishpat — Rabbis for Human Rights.* Married to Paula, a documentary filmmaker, they have three children: Zohar, Benjamin, and Raphaela.

ARNOLD JACOB WOLF

Rabbi Arnold Jacob Wolf was ordained at Hebrew Union College in 1948 with honors in theology and homiletics, and was later awarded a Doctorate of Divinity. He is responsible for more than two hundred fifty essays and five books, most recently *Jewish Spiritual Journeys* and *Unfinished Rabbi.* He was a founding editor of *Sh'ma: A Journal of Jewish Responsibility* and is presently an editor for *Judaism.* Rabbi Wolf is a board member of the Jewish Peace Fellowship, the Jewish Council on Urban Affairs, and other social action organizations. He was founding rabbi of the avant-garde Congregation Solel on Chicago's North Shore, and Jewish Chaplain at Yale University. Arnold Jacob Wolf is rabbi emeritus of K. A. M. Isaiah Israel in Chicago, Illinois, where he served as senior rabbi from 1980 to 1999.

Notes

Notes

Notes

Notes

Notes

Notes

Notes

Notes

About JEWISH LIGHTS Publishing

People of all faiths and backgrounds yearn for books that attract, engage, educate and spiritually inspire.

Our principal goal is to stimulate thought and help all people learn about who the Jewish People are, where they come from, and what the future can be made to hold. While people of our diverse Jewish heritage are the primary audience, our books speak to people in the Christian world as well and will broaden their understanding of Judaism and the roots of their own faith.

We bring to you authors who are at the forefront of spiritual thought and experience. While each has something different to say, they all say it in a voice that you can hear.

Our books are designed to welcome you and then to engage, stimulate and inspire. We judge our success not only by whether or not our books are beautiful and commercially successful, but by whether or not they make a difference in your life.

We at Jewish Lights take great care to produce beautiful books that present meaningful spiritual content in a form that reflects the art of making high quality books. Therefore, we want to acknowledge those who contributed to the production of this book.

Stuart M. Matlins, Publisher

PRODUCTION
Marian B. Wallace & Bridgett Taylor

EDITORIAL & PROOFREADING
Sandra Korinchak, Martha McKinney & Amanda Dupuis

JACKET DESIGN
Bridgett Taylor

TYPESETTING
Reuben Kantor, QEP Design, Jamaica Plain, Massachusetts

TEXT DESIGN
Josh Silverman, schwadesign, Cambridge, Massachusetts

JACKET / TEXT PRINTING AND BINDING
Lake Book, Melrose Park, Illinois

Spirituality

The Women's Torah Commentary: New Insights from Women Rabbis on the 54 Weekly Torah Portions Ed. by Rabbi Elyse Goldstein

For the first time, women rabbis provide a commentary on the entire Torah. More than 25 years after the first woman was ordained a rabbi in America, women have an impressive group of spiritual role models that they never had before. Here, in a week-by-week format, these inspiring teachers bring their rich perspectives to bear on the biblical text. A perfect gift for others, or for yourself. 6 x 9, 320 pp (est), HC, ISBN 1-58023-076-8 **$24.95** (Avail. April 2000)

Bringing the Psalms to Life
How to Understand and Use the Book of Psalms by Rabbi Daniel F. Polish

Here, the most beloved—and least understood—of the books in the Bible comes alive. This simultaneously insightful and practical guide shows how the Psalms address a myriad of spiritual issues in our lives: feeling abandoned, overcoming illness, dealing with anger, and more. 6 x 9, 208 pp (est), HC, ISBN 1-58023-077-6 **$21.95** (Avail. April 2000)

Stepping Stones to Jewish Spiritual Living: Walking the Path
Morning, Noon, and Night by Rabbi James L. Mirel & Karen Bonnell Werth

Transforms our daily routine into sacred acts of mindfulness. Chapters are arranged according to the cycle of each day. "A wonderful, practical, and inspiring guidebook to gently bring the riches of Jewish practice into our busy, everyday lives. Highly recommended." —Rabbi David A. Cooper. 6 x 9, 240 pp, Quality PB, ISBN 1-58023-074-1 **$16.95**; HC, ISBN 1-58023-003-2 **$21.95**

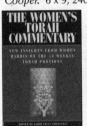 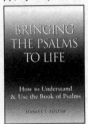 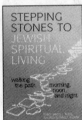 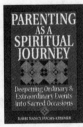 

Parenting As a Spiritual Journey:
Deepening Ordinary & Extraordinary Events into Sacred Occasions
by Rabbi Nancy Fuchs-Kreimer 6 x 9, 224 pp, Quality PB, ISBN 1-58023-016-4 **$16.95**

The Year Mom Got Religion: *One Woman's Midlife Journey into Judaism*
by Lee Meyerhoff Hendler 6 x 9, 208 pp, Quality PB, ISBN 1-58023-070-9 **$15.95**;
HC, ISBN 1-58023-000-8 **$19.95**

Moses—The Prince, the Prophet: *His Life, Legend & Message for Our Lives*
by Rabbi Levi Meier, Ph.D. 6 x 9, 224 pp, Quality PB, ISBN 1-58023-069-5 **$16.95**;
HC, ISBN 1-58023-013-X **$23.95**

Ancient Secrets: *Using the Stories of the Bible to Improve Our Everyday Lives*
by Rabbi Levi Meier, Ph.D. 5½ x 8½, 288 pp, Quality PB, ISBN 1-58023-064-4 **$16.95**

Or phone, fax or mail to: **JEWISH LIGHTS** Publishing
Sunset Farm Offices, Route 4 • P.O. Box 237 • Woodstock, Vermont 05091
Tel: (802) 457-4000 • Fax: (802) 457-4004 • www.jewishlights.com
Credit card orders: **(800) 962-4544** (9AM–5PM ET Monday–Friday)
Generous discounts on quantity orders. SATISFACTION GUARANTEED. Prices subject to change.

Spirituality & More

These Are the Words: *A Vocabulary of Jewish Spiritual Life*
by *Arthur Green*

What are the most essential ideas, concepts and terms that an educated person needs to know about Judaism? From *Adonai* (My Lord) to *zekhut* (merit), this enlightening and entertaining journey through Judaism teaches us the 149 core Hebrew words that constitute the basic vocabulary of Jewish spiritual life. 6 x 9, 304 pp, HC, ISBN 1-58023-024-5 **$21.95**

The Enneagram and Kabbalah: *Reading Your Soul*
by *Rabbi Howard A. Addison*

Combines two of the most powerful maps of consciousness known to humanity—The Tree of Life (the *Sefirot*) from the Jewish mystical tradition of *Kabbalah*, and the nine-pointed Enneagram—and shows how, together, they can provide a powerful tool for self-knowledge, critique, and transformation. 6 x 9, 176 pp, Quality PB, ISBN 1-58023-001-6 **$15.95**

Embracing the Covenant
Converts to Judaism Talk About Why & How
Ed. and with Intros. by *Rabbi Allan L. Berkowitz* and *Patti Moskovitz*

Through personal experiences of 20 converts to Judaism, this book illuminates reasons for converting, the quest for a satisfying spirituality, the appeal of the Jewish tradition and how conversion has changed lives—the convert's, and the lives of those close to them.
6 x 9, 192 pp, Quality PB, ISBN 1-879045-50-8 **$15.95**

Shared Dreams: *Martin Luther King, Jr., and the Jewish Community*
by Rabbi Marc Schneier; Intro. by Martin Luther King III
6 x 9, 240 pp, HC, ISBN 1-58023-062-8 **$24.95**

Mystery Midrash: *An Anthology of Jewish Mystery & Detective Fiction*
Ed. by Lawrence W. Raphael; Intro. by Joel Siegel, ABC's *Good Morning America*
6 x 9, 304 pp, Quality PB, ISBN 1-58023-55-5 **$16.95**

The Jewish Gardening Cookbook: *Growing Plants & Cooking for Holidays & Festivals*
by Michael Brown 6 x 9, 224 pp, HC, Illus., ISBN 1-58023-004-0 **$21.95**

Wandering Stars: *An Anthology of Jewish Fantasy & Science Fiction* Ed. by Jack Dann; Intro. by Isaac Asimov 6 x 9, 272 pp, Quality PB, ISBN 1-58023-005-9 **$16.95**

More Wandering Stars
An Anthology of Outstanding Stories of Jewish Fantasy & Science Fiction
Ed. by Jack Dann; Intro. by Isaac Asimov 6 x 9, 192 pp, Quality PB, ISBN 1-58023-063-6 **$16.95**

A Heart of Wisdom: *Making the Jewish Journey from Midlife through the Elder Years*
Ed. by Susan Berrin; Foreword by Harold Kushner
6 x 9, 384 pp, Quality PB, ISBN 1-58023-051-2 **$18.95**; HC, ISBN 1-879045-73-7 **$24.95**

Sacred Intentions: *Daily Inspiration to Strengthen the Spirit, Based on Jewish Wisdom*
by Rabbi Kerry M. Olitzky and Rabbi Lori Forman
4½ x 6½, 448 pp, Quality PB, ISBN 1-58023-061-X **$15.95**

Life Cycle & Holidays

How to Be a Perfect Stranger, In 2 Volumes
A Guide to Etiquette in Other People's Religious Ceremonies
Ed. by *Stuart M. Matlins* & *Arthur J. Magida* **AWARD WINNER!**

What will happen? What do I do? What do I wear? What do I say? What should I avoid doing, wearing, saying? What are their basic beliefs? Should I bring a gift? In question-and-answer format, *How to Be a Perfect Stranger* explains the rituals and celebrations of America's major religions/denominations, helping an interested guest to feel comfortable, participate to the fullest extent possible, and avoid violating anyone's religious principles. It is not a guide to theology, nor is it presented from the perspective of any particular faith.
Vol. 1: *America's Largest Faiths,* 6 x 9, 432 pp, HC, ISBN 1-879045-39-7 **$24.95**;
Vol. 2: *Other Faiths in America,* 6 x 9, 416 pp, HC, ISBN 1-879045-63-X **$24.95**

Putting God on the Guest List, 2nd Ed.
How to Reclaim the Spiritual Meaning of Your Child's Bar or Bat Mitzvah
by *Rabbi Jeffrey K. Salkin* **AWARD WINNER!**

The expanded, updated, revised edition of today's most influential book (over 60,000 copies in print) about finding core spiritual values in American Jewry's most misunderstood ceremony.
6 x 9, 224 pp, Quality PB, ISBN 1-879045-59-1 **$16.95**; HC, ISBN 1-879045-58-3 **$24.95**

For Kids—Putting God on Your Guest List
How to Claim the Spiritual Meaning of Your Bar or Bat Mitzvah
by Rabbi Jeffrey K. Salkin 6 x 9, 144 pp, Quality PB, ISBN 1-58023-015-6 **$14.95**

Bar/Bat Mitzvah Basics
A Practical Family Guide to Coming of Age Together
Ed. by Cantor Helen Leneman 6 x 9, 240 pp, Quality PB, ISBN 1-879045-54-0 **$16.95**;
HC, ISBN 1-879045-51-6 **$24.95**

The New Jewish Baby Book **AWARD WINNER!**
Names, Ceremonies, Customs—A Guide for Today's Families
by Anita Diamant 6 x 9, 336 pp, Quality PB, ISBN 1-879045-28-1 **$16.95**

Hanukkah: The Art of Jewish Living
by Dr. Ron Wolfson 7 x 9, 192 pp, Quality PB Original, Illus., ISBN 1-879045-97-4 **$16.95**

The Shabbat Seder: The Art of Jewish Living
by Dr. Ron Wolfson 7 x 9, 272 pp, Quality PB, Illus., ISBN 1-879045-90-7 **$16.95**
Also available are these helpful companions to *The Shabbat Seder*: Booklet of the Blessings and Songs, ISBN 1-879045-91-5 **$5.00**; Audiocassette of the Blessings, DN03 **$6.00**; Teacher's Guide, ISBN 1-879045-92-3 **$4.95**

The Passover Seder: The Art of Jewish Living
by Dr. Ron Wolfson 7 x 9, 336 pp, Quality PB, Illus., ISBN 1-879045-93-1 **$16.95**
Also available are these helpful companions to *The Passover Seder*: Booklet of the Blessings and Songs, ISBN 1-879045-94-X **$5.00**; Audiocassette of the Blessings, DN04 **$6.00**; Teacher's Guide, ISBN 1-879045-95-8 **$4.95**

Spirituality—The Kushner Series

Honey from the Rock, Special Anniversary Edition
An Introduction to Jewish Mysticism
by *Lawrence Kushner*

An insightful and absorbing introduction to the ten gates of Jewish mysticism and how it applies to daily life. "The easiest introduction to Jewish mysticism you can read."
6 x 9, 176 pp, Quality PB, ISBN 1-58023-073-3 **$15.95**

Eyes Remade for Wonder
The Way of Jewish Mysticism and Sacred Living
A Lawrence Kushner Reader

Intro. by *Thomas Moore*

Whether you are new to Kushner or a devoted fan, you'll find inspiration here. With samplings from each of Kushner's works, and a generous amount of new material, this book is to be read and reread, each time discovering deeper layers of meaning in our lives.
6 x 9, 240 pp, Quality PB, ISBN 1-58023-042-3 **$16.95**; HC, ISBN 1-58023-014-8 **$23.95**

Invisible Lines of Connection
Sacred Stories of the Ordinary
by *Lawrence Kushner* **AWARD WINNER!**

Through his everyday encounters with family, friends, colleagues and strangers, Kushner takes us deeply into our lives, finding flashes of spiritual insight in the process.
5½ x 8½, 160 pp, Quality PB, ISBN 1-879045-98-2 **$15.95**; HC, ISBN 1-879045-52-4 **$21.95**

The Book of Letters
A Mystical Hebrew Alphabet **AWARD WINNER!**
by Lawrence Kushner
Popular HC Edition, 6 x 9, 80 pp, 2-color text, ISBN 1-879045-00-1 **$24.95**; *Deluxe Gift Edition*, 9 x 12, 80 pp, HC, 2-color text, ornamentation, slipcase, ISBN 1-879045-01-X **$79.95**; *Collector's Limited Edition*, 9 x 12, 80 pp, HC, gold-embossed pages, hand-assembled slipcase. With silkscreened print. Limited to 500 signed and numbered copies, ISBN 1-879045-04-4 **$349.00**

The Book of Words
Talking Spiritual Life, Living Spiritual Talk **AWARD WINNER!**
by Lawrence Kushner 6 x 9, 160 pp, 2-color text, Quality PB, ISBN 1-58023-020-2 **$16.95**; HC, ISBN 1-879045-35-4 **$21.95**

God Was in This Place & I, i Did Not Know
Finding Self, Spirituality & Ultimate Meaning
by Lawrence Kushner 6 x 9, 192 pp, Quality PB, ISBN 1-879045-33-8 **$16.95**

The River of Light: *Spirituality, Judaism, Consciousness*
by Lawrence Kushner 6 x 9, 192 pp, Quality PB, ISBN 1-879045-03-6 **$14.95**

Healing/Wellness/Recovery

Jewish Pastoral Care
A Practical Handbook from Traditional and Contemporary Sources
Ed. by *Rabbi Dayle A. Friedman*

This innovative resource builds on the classic foundations of pastoral care, enriching it with uniquely Jewish traditions and wisdom. Gives today's Jewish pastoral counselors practical guidelines based in the Jewish tradition. 6 x 9, 352 pp (est), HC, ISBN 1-58023-078-4 **$34.95** (Avail. May 2000)

Healing of Soul, Healing of Body
Spiritual Leaders Unfold the Strength & Solace in Psalms
Ed. by *Rabbi Simkha Y. Weintraub, CSW*, for The Jewish Healing Center

A source of solace for those who are facing illness, as well as those who care for them. Provides a wellspring of strength with inspiring introductions and commentaries by eminent spiritual leaders reflecting all Jewish movements. 6 x 9, 128 pp, Quality PB, Illus., 2-color text, ISBN 1-879045-31-1 **$14.95**

Self, Struggle & Change: *Family Conflict Stories in Genesis and Their Healing Insights for Our Lives*
by *Dr. Norman J. Cohen*

How do I find wholeness in my life and in my family's life? Here a modern master of biblical interpretation brings us greater understanding of the ancient text and of ourselves in this intriguing re-telling of conflict between husband and wife, father and son, brothers and sisters. 6 x 9, 224 pp, Quality PB, ISBN 1-879045-64-4 **$16.95**; HC, ISBN 1-879045-19-2 **$21.95**

Twelve Jewish Steps to Recovery: *A Personal Guide to Turning from Alcoholism & Other Addictions . . . Drugs, Food, Gambling, Sex . . .* by Rabbi Kerry M. Olitzky & Stuart A. Copans, M.D. Preface by Abraham J. Twerski, M.D.; Intro. by Rabbi Sheldon Zimmerman; "Getting Help"by JACS Foundation 6 x 9, 144 pp, Quality PB, ISBN 1-879045-09-5 **$13.95**

One Hundred Blessings Every Day: *Daily Twelve Step Recovery Affirmations, Exercises for Personal Growth & Renewal Reflecting Seasons of the Jewish Year* by Rabbi Kerry M. Olitzky, with selected meditations prepared by Rabbi James Stone Goodman, Danny Siegel, and Gordon Tucker. Foreword by Rabbi Neil Gillman, The Jewish Theological Seminary of America; Afterword by Dr. Jay Holder, Director, Exodus Treatment Center 4½ x 6½, 432 pp, Quality PB, ISBN 1-879045-30-3 **$14.95**

Recovery from Codependence: *A Jewish Twelve Steps Guide to Healing Your Soul* by Rabbi Kerry M. Olitzky; Foreword by Marc Galanter, M.D., Director, Division of Alcoholism & Drug Abuse, NYU Medical Center; Afterword by Harriet Rossetto, Director, Gateways Beit T'shuvah 6 x 9, 160 pp, Quality PB, ISBN 1-879045-32-X **$13.95**; HC, ISBN 1-879045-27-3 **$21.95**

Renewed Each Day: *Daily Twelve Step Recovery Meditations Based on the Bible* by Rabbi Kerry M. Olitzky & Aaron Z. *Vol. I: Genesis & Exodus*; Intro. by Rabbi Michael A. Signer; Afterword by JACS Foundation. *Vol. II: Leviticus, Numbers and Deuteronomy*; Introduction by Sharon M. Strassfeld; Afterword by Rabbi Harold M. Schulweis
Vol. I: 6 x 9, 224 pp, Quality PB, ISBN 1-879045-12-5 **$14.95**;
Vol. II: 6 x 9, 280 pp, Quality PB, ISBN 1-879045-13-3 **$14.95**

Children's Spirituality

A Prayer for the Earth
The Story of Naamah, Noah's Wife
by *Sandy Eisenberg Sasso*
Full color illus. by *Bethanne Andersen*

**For ages
4 & up**

NONDENOMINATIONAL, NONSECTARIAN

This new story, based on an ancient text, opens readers' religious imaginations to new ideas about the well-known story of the Flood. When God tells Noah to bring the animals of the world onto the ark, God also calls on Naamah, Noah's wife, to save each plant on Earth.

"A lovely tale. . . . Children of all ages should be drawn to this parable for our times."
                    —*Tomie dePaola*, artist/author of books for children
9 x 12, 32 pp, HC, Full-color illus., ISBN 1-879045-60-5 **$16.95**

The 11th Commandment: Wisdom from Our Children
by The Children of America

For all ages

MULTICULTURAL, NONDENOMINATIONAL, NONSECTARIAN

"If there were an Eleventh Commandment, what would it be?" Children of many religious denominations across America answer this question—in their own drawings and words. "A rare book of spiritual celebration for all people, of all ages, for all time."—*Bookviews*
8 x 10, 48 pp. HC, Full-color illus., ISBN 1-879045-46-X **$16.95**

Sharing Blessings: Children's Stories for Exploring the Spirit of the Jewish Holidays
by *Rahel Musleah* and *Rabbi Michael Klayman*
Full-color illus. by *Mary O'Keefe Young*

**For ages
6 & up**

What is the spiritual message of each of the Jewish holidays? How do we teach it to our children? Many books tell children about the historical significance and customs of the holidays. Now, through engaging, creative stories about one family's preparation, *Sharing Blessings* explores ways to get into the *spirit* of 13 different holidays. "Lighthearted, and yet thorough—allows all Jewish parents (even those with very little Jewish education) to introduce the spirit of our cherished holiday traditions." —*Shari Lewis*, creator and star of PBS' *Lamb Chop's Play-Along*
7 x 10, 64 pp, HC, Full-color illus., ISBN 1-879045-71-0 **$18.95**

The Book of Miracles
A Young Person's Guide to Jewish Spiritual Awareness
by *Lawrence Kushner*

**For ages
9 & up**

From the miracle at the Red Sea to the miracle of waking up this morning, this intriguing book introduces kids to a way of everyday spiritual thinking to last a lifetime. Kushner, whose award-winning books have brought spirituality to life for countless adults, now shows young people how to use Judaism as a foundation on which to build their lives. "A well-written, easy to understand, very lovely guide to Jewish spirituality. I recommend it to all teens as a good read." —*Kimberly Kirberger*, co-author, *Chicken Soup for the Teenage Soul* 6 x 9, 96 pp, HC, 2-color illus., ISBN 1-879045-78-8 **$16.95**

Children's Spirituality

In Our Image
God's First Creatures

For ages 4 & up

by *Nancy Sohn Swartz*
Full-color illus. by *Melanie Hall*
NONDENOMINATIONAL, NONSECTARIAN

A playful new twist on the Creation story—from the perspective of the animals. Celebrates the interconnectedness of nature and the harmony of all living things. "The vibrantly colored illustrations nearly leap off the page in this delightful interpretation." —*School Library Journal*

"A message all children should hear, presented in words and pictures that children will find irresistible." —*Rabbi Harold Kushner*, author of *When Bad Things Happen to Good People*

9 x 12, 32 pp, HC, Full color illus., ISBN 1-879045-99-0 **$16.95**

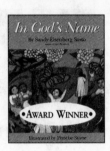

God's Paintbrush

For ages 4 & up

by *Sandy Eisenberg Sasso*; Full color illus. by *Annette Compton*
MULTICULTURAL, NONDENOMINATIONAL, NONSECTARIAN

Invites children of all faiths and backgrounds to encounter God openly in their own lives. Wonderfully interactive; provides questions adult and child can explore together at the end of each episode. "An excellent way to honor the imaginative breadth and depth of the spiritual life of the young." —*Dr. Robert Coles*, Harvard University
11 x 8½, 32 pp, HC, Full color illus., ISBN 1-879045-22-2 **$16.95**

Also available: A Teacher's Guide: A Guide for Jewish & Christian Educators and Parents 8½ x 11, 32 pp, PB, ISBN 1-879045-57-5 **$6.95**

God's Paintbrush Celebration Kit 8½ x 11, HC, Includes 5 sessions/40 full color Activity Sheets and Teacher Folder with complete instructions, ISBN 1-58023-050-4 **$21.95**

In God's Name

For ages 4 & up

by *Sandy Eisenberg Sasso*; Full-color illus. by *Phoebe Stone*
MULTICULTURAL, NONDENOMINATIONAL, NONSECTARIAN

Like an ancient myth in its poetic text and vibrant illustrations, this award-winning modern fable about the search for God's name celebrates the diversity and, at the same time, the unity of all the people of the world. "What a lovely, healing book!" —*Madeleine L'Engle*
9 x 12, 32 pp, HC, Full color illus., ISBN 1-879045-26-5 **$16.95**

What Is God's Name? (A Board Book)

For ages 0–4

An abridged board book version of the award-winning *In God's Name.*
5 x 5, 24 pp, Board, Full color illus., ISBN 1-893361-10-1 **$7.95**

Children's Spirituality

God Said Amen
by *Sandy Eisenberg Sasso*
Full-color illus. by *Avi Katz*

For ages 4 & up

MULTICULTURAL, NONDENOMINATIONAL, NONSECTARIAN

A warm and inspiring tale of two kingdoms: Midnight Kingdom is overflowing with water but has no oil to light its lamps; Desert Kingdom is blessed with oil but has no water to grow its gardens. The kingdoms' rulers ask God for help but are too stubborn to ask each other. It takes a minstrel, a pair of royal riding-birds and their young keepers, and a simple act of kindness to show that they need only reach out to each other to find the answers to their prayers.

9 x 12, 32 pp, HC, Full color illus., ISBN 1-58023-080-6 **$16.95**

For Heaven's Sake
by *Sandy Eisenberg Sasso*; Full-color illus. by *Kathryn Kunz Finney*

For ages 4 & up

MULTICULTURAL, NONDENOMINATIONAL, NONSECTARIAN

Everyone talked about heaven: "Thank heavens." "Heaven forbid." "For heaven's sake, Isaiah." But no one would say what heaven was or how to find it. So Isaiah decides to find out, by seeking answers from many different people. "This book is a reminder of how well Sandy Sasso knows the minds of children. But it may surprise—and delight—readers to find how well she knows us grown-ups too." —*Maria Harris*, National Consultant in Religious Education, and author of *Teaching and Religious Imagination* 9 x 12, 32 pp, HC, Full color illus., ISBN 1-58023-054-7 **$16.95**

But God Remembered: Stories of Women from Creation to the Promised Land
by *Sandy Eisenberg Sasso*; Full-color illus. by *Bethanne Andersen*

For ages 8 & up

NONDENOMINATIONAL, NONSECTARIAN

A fascinating collection of four different stories of women only briefly mentioned in biblical tradition and religious texts. Award-winning author Sasso vibrantly brings to life courageous and strong women from ancient tradition; all teach important values through their actions and faith. "Exquisite. . . . A book of beauty, strength and spirituality." —*Association of Bible Teachers* 9 x 12, 32 pp, HC, Full color illus., ISBN 1-879045-43-5 **$16.95**

God in Between
by *Sandy Eisenberg Sasso*; Full color illus. by *Sally Sweetland*

For ages 4 & up

MULTICULTURAL, NONDENOMINATIONAL, NONSECTARIAN

If you wanted to find God, where would you look? A magical, mythical tale that teaches that God can be found where we are: within all of us and the relationships between us. "This happy and wondrous book takes our children on a sweet and holy journey into God's presence." —*Rabbi Wayne Dosick, Ph.D.*, author of *Golden Rules* and *Soul Judaism*
9 x 12, 32 pp, HC, Full color illus., ISBN 1-879045-86-9 **$16.95**

Spirituality

My People's Prayer Book: *Traditional Prayers, Modern Commentaries*

Ed. by *Dr. Lawrence A. Hoffman*

This momentous, critically-acclaimed series is truly a people's prayer book, one that provides a diverse and exciting commentary to the traditional liturgy. It will help modern men and women find new wisdom and guidance in Jewish prayer, and bring liturgy into their lives. Each book includes Hebrew text, modern translation, and commentaries *from all perspectives* of the Jewish world. Vol. 1—*The Sh'ma and Its Blessings,* 7 x 10, 168 pp, HC, ISBN 1-879045-79-6 **$23.95**
Vol. 2—*The Amidah,* 7 x 10, 240 pp, HC ISBN 1-879045-80-X **$21.95**
Vol. 3—*P'sukei D'zimrah* (Morning Psalms), 7 x 10, 240 pp, HC, ISBN 1-879045-81-8 **$21.95**
Vol. 4—*Seder K'riyat Hatorah* (Shabbat Torah Service), 7 x 10, 240 pp, ISBN 1-879045-82-6 **$23.95**
(Avail. April 2000)

Voices from Genesis: *Guiding Us through the Stages of Life*

by *Dr. Norman J. Cohen*

In a brilliant blending of modern *midrash* (finding contemporary meaning from biblical texts) and the life stages of Erik Erikson's developmental psychology, the characters of Genesis come alive to give us insights for our own journeys. 6 x 9, 192 pp, HC, ISBN 1-879045-75-3 **$21.95**

   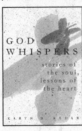 

God Whispers: *Stories of the Soul, Lessons of the Heart*
by Rabbi Karyn D. Kedar 6 x 9, 176 pp, HC, ISBN 1-58023-023-7 **$19.95**

Being God's Partner
How to Find the Hidden Link Between Spirituality and Your Work AWARD WINNER!
by Rabbi Jeffrey K. Salkin; Intro. by Norman Lear
6 x 9, 192 pp, Quality PB, ISBN 1-879045-65-6 **$16.95**; HC, 1-879045-37-0 **$19.95**

ReVisions: *Seeing Torah through a Feminist Lens* AWARD WINNER!
by Rabbi Elyse Goldstein 5½ x 8½, 208 pp, HC, ISBN 1-58023-047-4 **$19.95**

Soul Judaism: *Dancing with God into a New Era*
by Rabbi Wayne Dosick 5½ x 8½, 304 pp, Quality PB, ISBN 1-58023-053-9 **$16.95**

Finding Joy: *A Practical Spiritual Guide to Happiness* AWARD WINNER!
by Rabbi Dannel I. Schwartz with Mark Hass
6 x 9, 192 pp, Quality PB, ISBN 1-58023-009-1 **$14.95**; HC, ISBN 1-879045-53-2 **$19.95**

The Empty Chair: *Finding Hope and Joy—*
Timeless Wisdom from a Hasidic Master, Rebbe Nachman of Breslov AWARD WINNER!
Adapted by Moshe Mykoff and the Breslov Research Institute
4 x 6, 128 pp, 2-color text, Deluxe PB, ISBN 1-879045-67-2 **$9.95**

The Gentle Weapon: *Prayers for Everyday and Not-So-Everyday Moments*
Adapted from the Wisdom of Rebbe Nachman of Breslov by Moshe Mykoff and
S. C. Mizrahi, with the Breslov Research Institute
4 x 6, 144 pp, 2-color text, Deluxe PB, ISBN 1-58023-022-9 **$9.95**

"Who Is a Jew?" *Conversations, Not Conclusions* by Merle Hyman
6 x 9, 272 pp, Quality PB, ISBN 1-58023-052-0 **$16.95**; HC, ISBN 1-879045-76-1 **$23.95**

Life Cycle

Jewish Paths toward Healing and Wholeness
A Personal Guide to Dealing With Suffering
by *Rabbi Kerry M. Olitzky*

"Why me?" Why do we suffer? How can we heal? Grounded in the spiritual traditions of Judaism, this book provides healing rituals, psalms and prayers that help readers initiate a dialogue with God, to guide them along the complicated path of healing and wholeness.
6 x 9, 192 pp (est), Quality PB, ISBN 1-58023-068-7 **$15.95** (Avail. May 2000)

Mourning & Mitzvah: *A Guided Journal for Walking the Mourner's Path through Grief to Healing*
by *Anne Brener*, L.C.S.W.; Foreword by *Rabbi Jack Riemer*; Intro. by *Rabbi William Cutter*

For those who mourn a death, for those who would help them, for those who face a loss of any kind, Brener teaches us the power and strength available to us in the fully experienced mourning process. 7½ x 9, 288 pp, Quality PB, ISBN 1-879045-23-0 **$19.95**

Tears of Sorrow, Seeds of Hope
A Jewish Spiritual Companion for Infertility and Pregnancy Loss
by *Rabbi Nina Beth Cardin*

A spiritual companion that enables us to mourn infertility, a lost pregnancy, or a stillbirth within the prayers, rituals, and meditations of Judaism. By drawing on the texts of tradition, it creates readings and rites of mourning, and through them provides a wellspring of compassion, solace—and hope. 6 x 9, 192 pp, HC, ISBN 1-58023-017-2 **$19.95**

Lifecycles
V. 1: *Jewish Women on Life Passages & Personal Milestones* AWARD WINNER!
Ed. and with Intros. by Rabbi Debra Orenstein
V. 2: *Jewish Women on Biblical Themes in Contemporary Life* AWARD WINNER!
Ed. and with Intros. by Rabbi Debra Orenstein and Rabbi Jane Rachel Litman
V. 1: 6 x 9, 480 pp, Quality PB, ISBN 1-58023-018-0 **$19.95**; HC, ISBN 1-879045-14-1 **$24.95**
V. 2: 6 x 9, 464 pp, Quality PB, ISBN 1-58023-019-9 **$19.95**; HC, ISBN 1-879045-15-X **$24.95**

Grief in Our Seasons: *A Mourner's Kaddish Companion*
by Rabbi Kerry M. Olitzky 4½ x 6½, 448 pp, Quality PB, ISBN 1-879045-55-9 **$15.95**

A Time to Mourn, A Time to Comfort: *A Guide to Jewish Bereavement and Comfort*
by Dr. Ron Wolfson 7 x 9, 192 pp, Quality PB, ISBN 1-879045-33-8 **$16.95**

When a Grandparent Dies
A Kid's Own Remembering Workbook for Dealing with Shiva and the Year Beyond
by Nechama Liss-Levinson, Ph.D.
8 x 10, 48 pp, HC, Illus., 2-color text, ISBN 1-879045-44-3 **$15.95**

So That Your Values Live On: *Ethical Wills & How to Prepare Them*
Ed. by Rabbi Jack Riemer & Professor Nathaniel Stampfer
6 x 9, 272 pp, Quality PB, ISBN 1-879045-34-6 **$17.95**

Theology/Philosophy

A Heart of Many Rooms
Celebrating the Many Voices within Judaism
by *Dr. David Hartman* AWARD WINNER!

Named a *Publishers Weekly* "Best Book of the Year." Addresses the spiritual and theological questions that face all Jews and all people today. From the perspective of traditional Judaism, Hartman shows that commitment to both Jewish tradition and to pluralism can create understanding between people of different religious convictions.
6 x 9, 352 pp., HC, ISBN 1-58023-048-2 **$24.95**

A Living Covenant: *The Innovative Spirit in Traditional Judaism*
by *Dr. David Hartman* AWARD WINNER!

Winner, National Jewish Book Award. Hartman reveals a Judaism grounded in covenant—a relational framework—informed by the metaphor of marital love rather than that of parent-child dependency. 6 x 9, 368 pp, Quality PB, ISBN 1-58023-011-3 **$18.95**

The Death of Death: *Resurrection and Immortality in Jewish Thought*
by *Dr. Neil Gillman* AWARD WINNER!

Does death end life, or is it the passage from one stage of life to another? This National Jewish Book Award Finalist explores the original and compelling argument that Judaism, a religion often thought to pay little attention to the afterlife, not only offers us rich ideas on the subject—but delivers a deathblow to death itself. 6 x 9, 336 pp, Quality PB, ISBN 1-879045-87-7 **$18.95**; HC, ISBN 1-879045-61-3 **$23.95**

 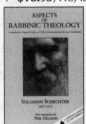   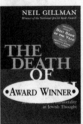

Aspects of Rabbinic Theology by Solomon Schechter; New Intro. by Dr. Neil Gillman
6 x 9, 448 pp, Quality PB, ISBN 1-879045-24-9 **$19.95**

The Last Trial: *On the Legends and Lore of the Command to Abraham to Offer Isaac as a Sacrifice* by Shalom Spiegel; New Intro. by Judah Goldin
6 x 9, 208 pp, Quality PB, ISBN 1-879045-29-X **$17.95**

Judaism and Modern Man: *An Interpretation of Jewish Religion* by Will Herberg; New Intro. by Dr. Neil Gillman 6 x 9, 336 pp, Quality PB, ISBN 1-879045-87-7 **$18.95**

Seeking the Path to Life AWARD WINNER!
Theological Meditations on God and the Nature of People, Love, Life and Death
by Rabbi Ira F. Stone
6 x 9, 160 pp, Quality PB, ISBN 1-879045-47-8 **$14.95**; HC, ISBN 1-879045-17-6 **$19.95**

The Spirit of Renewal: *Finding Faith after the Holocaust* AWARD WINNER!
by Rabbi Edward Feld
6 x 9, 224 pp, Quality PB, ISBN 1-879045-40-0 **$16.95**

Tormented Master: *The Life and Spiritual Quest of Rabbi Nahman of Bratslav*
by Dr. Arthur Green
6 x 9, 416 pp, Quality PB, ISBN 1-879045-11-7 **$18.95**

Your Word Is Fire: *The Hasidic Masters on Contemplative Prayer*
Ed. and Trans. with a New Introduction by Dr. Arthur Green and Dr. Barry W. Holtz
6 x 9, 160 pp, Quality PB, ISBN 1-879045-25-7 **$14.95**

Theology/Philosophy

Torah of the Earth: *Exploring 4,000 Years of Ecology in Jewish Thought*
Ed. by *Rabbi Arthur Waskow*

Major new resource offering us an invaluable key to understanding the intersection of ecology and Judaism. Leading scholars provide us with a guided tour of ecological thought from four major Jewish viewpoints. Vol. 1: *Biblical Israel & Rabbinic Judaism*, 6 x 9, 272 pp, Quality PB Original, ISBN 1-58023-086-5 **$19.95**; Vol. 2: *Zionism & Eco-Judaism*, 6 x 9, 272 pp, Quality PB Original, ISBN 1-58023-087-3 **$19.95** (Avail. May 2000)

Broken Tablets: *Restoring the Ten Commandments and Ourselves*
Ed. by *Rabbi Rachel S. Mikva*; Intro. by *Rabbi Lawrence Kushner*;
Afterword by *Rabbi Arnold Jacob Wolf* AWARD WINNER!

Twelve outstanding spiritual leaders each share profound and personal thoughts about these biblical commands and why they have such a special hold on us.
6 x 9, 208 pp, HC, ISBN 1-58023-066-0 **$21.95**

Evolving Halakhah: *A Progressive Approach to Traditional Jewish Law*
by *Rabbi Dr. Moshe Zemer*

Innovative and provocative, this book affirms the system of traditional Jewish law, *halakhah*, as flexible enough to accommodate the changing realities of each generation. It shows that the traditional framework for understanding the Torah's commandments can be the living heart of Jewish life for all Jews. 6 x 9, 480 pp, HC, ISBN 1-58023-002-4 **$40.00**

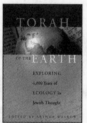  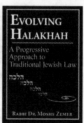  

God & the Big Bang
Discovering Harmony Between Science & Spirituality AWARD WINNER!
by Daniel C. Matt
6 x 9, 216 pp, Quality PB, ISBN 1-879045-89-3 **$16.95**; HC, ISBN 1-879045-48-6 **$21.95**

Israel—A Spiritual Travel Guide AWARD WINNER!
A Companion for the Modern Jewish Pilgrim
by Rabbi Lawrence A. Hoffman 4¾ x 10, 256 pp, Quality PB, ISBN 1-879045-56-7 **$18.95**

Godwrestling—Round 2: *Ancient Wisdom, Future Paths* AWARD WINNER!
by Rabbi Arthur Waskow
6 x 9, 352 pp, Quality PB, ISBN 1-879045-72-9 **$18.95**; HC, ISBN 1-879045-45-1 **$23.95**

Ecology & the Jewish Spirit: *Where Nature & the Sacred Meet* Ed. and with Intros.
by Ellen Bernstein 6 x 9, 288 pp, Quality PB, ISBN 1-58023-082-2 **$16.95**;
HC, ISBN 1-879045-88-5 **$23.95**

Israel: *An Echo of Eternity* by Abraham Joshua Heschel; New Intro. by
Dr. Susannah Heschel 5½ x 8, 272 pp, Quality PB, ISBN 1-879045-70-2 **$18.95**

The Earth Is the Lord's: *The Inner World of the Jew in Eastern Europe*
by Abraham Joshua Heschel 5½ x 8, 112 pp, Quality PB, ISBN 1-879045-42-7 **$13.95**

A Passion for Truth: *Despair and Hope in Hasidism* by Abraham Joshua Heschel
5½ x 8, 352 pp, Quality PB, ISBN 1-879045-41-9 $ **$18.95**

The Way Into... Series

A major 14-volume series to be completed over the next three years, *The Way Into...* provides an accessible and usable "guided tour" of the Jewish faith, its people, its history and beliefs—in total, an introduction to Judaism for adults that will permit them to understand and interact with sacred texts.

Each volume is written by a major modern scholar and teacher, and is organized around an important concept of Judaism.

The Way Into... will enable all readers to achieve a real sense of Jewish cultural literacy through guided study. Forthcoming volumes include:

The Way Into Torah

by *Dr. Norman J. Cohen*

What is "Torah"? What are the different approaches to studying Torah? What are the different levels of understanding Torah? For whom is the study intended? Explores the origins and development of Torah, why it should be studied and how to do it. Addresses these and many other issues in this easy-to-use, easy-to-understand introduction to the ancient subject.

6 x 9, 160 pp. (est), HC, ISBN 1-58023-028-8 **$19.95** (Avail. June 2000)

The Way Into Jewish Prayer

by *Dr. Lawrence A. Hoffman*

Explores the reasons for and the ways of Jewish prayer. Opens the door to 3,000 years of the Jewish way to God by making available all you need to feel at home in Jewish worship. Provides basic definitions of the terms you need to know as well as thoughtful analysis of the depth that lies beneath Jewish prayer.

6 x 9, 160 pp (est), HC, ISBN 1-58023-027-X **$19.95** (Avail. July 2000)

The Way Into Encountering God in Judaism

by *Dr. Neil Gillman*

Explains how Jews have encountered God throughout history—and today—by exploring the many metaphors for God in Jewish tradition. Explores the Jewish tradition's passionate but also conflicting ways of relating to God as Creator, relational partner, and a force in history and nature.

6 x 9, 176 pp (est), HC, ISBN 1-58023-025-3 **$19.95** (Avail. July 2000)

The Way Into Jewish Mystical Tradition

by *Rabbi Lawrence Kushner*

Explains the principles of Jewish mystical thinking, their religious and spiritual significance, and how they relate to our lives. A book that allows us to experience and understand the Jewish mystical approach to our place in the world.

6 x 9, 176 pp (est), HC, ISBN 1-58023-029-6 **$19.95** (Avail. July 2000)

Jewish Meditation

Discovering Jewish Meditation
Instruction & Guidance for Learning an Ancient Spiritual Practice
by *Nan Fink Gefen*

Gives readers of any level of understanding the tools to learn the practice of Jewish meditation on your own, starting you on the path to a deep spiritual and personal connection to God and to greater insight about your life. 6 x 9, 208 pp, Quality PB, ISBN 1-58023-067-9 **$16.95**

Meditation from the Heart of Judaism: *Today's Teachers Share Their Practices, Techniques, and Faith* Ed. by *Avram Davis*

A "how-to"guide for both beginning and experienced meditators, drawing on the wisdom of 22 masters of meditation who explain why and how they meditate. A detailed compendium of the experts' "best practices" offers advice and starting points. 6 x 9, 256 pp, Quality PB, ISBN 1-58023-049-0 **$16.95**; HC, ISBN 1-879045-77-X **$21.95**

The Way of Flame
A Guide to the Forgotten Mystical Tradition of Jewish Meditation
by *Avram Davis* 4½ x 8, 176 pp, Quality PB, ISBN 1-58023-060-1 **$15.95**

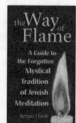

Entering the Temple of Dreams: *Jewish Prayers, Movements, and Meditations for the End of the Day* by *Tamar Frankiel* and *Judy Greenfeld*

Nighttime spirituality is much more than bedtime prayers! Here, you'll uncover deeper meaning to familiar nighttime prayers—and learn to combine the prayers with movements and meditations to enhance your physical and psychological wellbeing.
7 x 10, 184 pp (est), Illus., Quality PB, ISBN 1-58023-079-2 **$16.95** (Avail. April 2000)

Minding the Temple of the Soul: *Balancing Body, Mind, and Spirit through Traditional Jewish Prayer, Movement, and Meditation*

by *Tamar Frankiel* and *Judy Greenfeld*

This new spiritual approach to physical health introduces readers to a spiritual tradition that affirms the body and enables them to reconceive their bodies in a more positive light. Focuses on traditional Jewish prayers, with exercises, movements, and meditations. 7 x 10, 184 pp, Quality PB, Illus., ISBN 1-879045-64-8 **$16.95**; Audiotape of the Blessings, Movements and Meditations (60-min. cassette) **$16.95** Videotape of the Movements and Meditations (46-min. VHS) **$20.00**

Or phone, fax or mail to: **JEWISH LIGHTS Publishing**
Sunset Farm Offices, Route 4 • P.O. Box 237 • Woodstock, Vermont 05091
Tel (802) 457-4000   Fax (802) 457-4004   www.jewishlights.com
Credit card orders (800) 962-4544 (9AM–5PM ET Monday–Friday)
Generous discounts on quantity orders. SATISFACTION GUARANTEED. Prices subject to change.